OUR LADY

OF

UNITY

Her Community

Order this book online at www.trafford.com
or email orders@trafford.com

Most Trafford titles are also available at major online book retailers.

King James Version (KJV)
Public Domain

Print information available on the last page.

ISBN: 978-1-4907-8777-0 (sc)
ISBN: 978-1-4907-8782-4 (e)

Trafford rev. 03/13/2018

www.trafford.com
North America & international
toll-free: 1 888 232 4444 (USA & Canada)
fax: 812 355 4082

Nihil Obstat: Federico C. Garingo, O.L.O.U.
Censor Deputatus

Imprimatur: Rocade
Apostolic Administrator
Turlock, California
April 11, 2018

DEDICATED

to

The Most HOLY TRINITY

through

Our Lady of Unity

To: _____

From: _____

OURLADY'SPRESS

Our Lady of Unity

Many have ignored my Son's invitation to follow Him so they will obtain His marvelous promises. I am filled with sorrow that my redeemed children have wasted that one and only opportunity by choosing the wide path leading to eternal destruction. I was on the foot of the cross when my Son gave up His life so you can receive His divinity and to share His glory and splendor in the kingdom of heaven. As my Son had given all of Himself to you, I must also embrace you as my very own. I am God's gift to you. Accept me as your mother for I am called Mother of Perpetual Help and always waiting for you. Even though I am now gloriously crown as queen of heaven and earth, I remain sorrowful knowing that there is that greatest need of conversion for all my children.

In 1917, in Portugal, the world saw the sun spun as I appeared to the three little children at Fatima revealing to them the great need of repentance and for the conversion of the world. I let them saw what hell is like. I made known to the world that every day thousands and thousands of souls were lost and many accepted my message of prayers and repentance. On that day the world was changed but as the years passed many reverted to the old ways by choosing to be irreligious and godless. The wide road of perdition expanded wider than ever as more souls were lost each day that I have to keep appearing to many places.

"Many men in this world afflict the Lord. I desire souls to console Him to soften the anger of the heavenly Father. I wish, with my Son, for souls who will repair by their suffering and their poverty for the sinners and ingrates."

This was my message when I appeared in 1973 at Akita, Japan. It was a glorious day for it gathered and brought many back to the true church and many offered themselves for the conversion of the world.

A hundred years later after my appearance at Fatima the world has gotten so worst despite the good efforts of my Son's servants in preaching and teaching the Gospel. Billions heard the proclamation of my Son's Gospel but the hearts remain cold and hard grieving us even more than before. I even shed tears of blood in some of my appearances replicating my Son's precious blood poured at Calvary reminding all how precious and priceless your redemption. If you only knew and saw everything my Son did for you then you will surely be faithful and true to Him in appreciation for giving His love and life for your greatest and highest good.

Our Lady revealed to the community that she needed more help in helping our Lord in drawing and inspiring more souls to generously give themselves as consecrated and professed member of Her Order for the conversion of billions of souls so they can enter His kingdom. She called us to become co-workers in our Lord's vineyard to compensate the loss of many souls. Our Lady knew her calling was always to intercede for us for our conversion and salvation. On the cross our Lord called His mother as He was about to expire.

"Woman behold thy Son." (John 19:26). Our Lady saw how horrific and terrifying was the suffering our Lord endured on the cross and Jesus knew how His own mother suffered and there never be such sorrow as hers. The heart of Mary was pierced by a sword but worst, it penetrated to her soul and spirit. We can never felt her sorrow for our love for her Son is negligible. She does not want Jesus to die but her will was always in conformity to God. Against her own will Mary accepted her Son's death knowing that it was His mission to suffer and to die for the redemption of the world and for the salvation of all souls.

As she looked at her dying Son, Mary understood why Jesus called her. The Third Persona of God, Mary's Spouse revealed to her that she was greatly needed by Jesus to be His first follower, first disciple, first apostle, first evangelist and the first who must remind us that we are now free to enter the kingdom of heaven by the working of her Son. Mary also knew that God created her specially to be His greatest intercessor and partner with His Second Persona in order to accomplish His greatest work. Mary also knew that she was always one with the Holy Trinity and she alone understood why God must have His Three Persona. Our Lady knew that God destined her to be the new ark of the covenant which will carry God's children into the new heaven. God protected and preserved Mary from the stain of original sin so her womb that will carry the most

High God will be keep holy. The holy God will never set foot on a womb stained with sin.

"Hail Mary full of grace." The archangel Gabriel saluted her knowing that God gave Mary the greatest grace a creature will ever receive that is the fullness of God. Mary received not only one but His three Persons so she can fully participate with her Son in redeeming us thus Mary deserves the title, Co-Redeemer.

"My soul proclaims the greatness of the Lord." She rejoiced knowing how God loved and favored her showering this little lamb with all His graces so she will succeed in fulfilling God's plan in restoring and recreating us to become a true and real children of the Most High through Jesus Christ, Mary's only Son.

"Son behold thy mother." (John 19:27).

We are called by God to imitate our Lady's life so we too can receive the fullness of His grace thus together with her we too can proclaim the greatness of the Lord and the future generation will call us blessed for God the Almighty indeed has done great things for us.

Despite of such lofty guaranteed promises of eternal happiness and unending joy to those who listen and follow Him, hearts remain colder and harder, ears remain deafer and deafer and eyes remain blinder and blinder that I called a chosen few to be my messenger so the world will respond by truly and really appreciating and embracing what God had done for us and to make radical changes with their lives. My chosen ones received the Order to devote and dedicate themselves in teaching and inspiring the world how to effectually console and comfort the sorrows of the God of Abraham by knowing, loving and serving His Three Persona.

Professed and consecrated members of my community will continue to receive and follow the Order design to bring unity to all God's people and its mission will continue till the world ends.

Introduction

The word of God is spirit and life bringing many to a new life with Christ as the standard bearer showing the way, the truth and the life. All who followed Christ were called Christians and many were drawn to His lofty teaching and to His promise that all who believes in Him will have eternal life. Billions of copies of Sacred Scriptures are scattered all over the world spreading the seed of divinity so its growth can be manifested in every living soul.

Indeed, the Spirit of God is working in us as Christian churches are expanding rapidly all over the world inspiring billions of followers to follow the Son of God. Also, billions more are drawn to other religion which is indicative that truly God is at work calling all His creation to come and enter into an intimate relationship with the Most High by knowing and serving Him. Such sacred events does pleases God but the sad fact remains that still so many souls are lost everyday.

Why?

"For I say unto you, that except your righteousness shall exceed the righteousness of the scribes and Pharisees, ye shall in no case enter into the kingdom of heaven." (Matthew 5:20).

The scribes and the Pharisees were prime example of the religious. The scribes knew all about the letter of the law and the Pharisees practices what is prescribed by the law. In the gathering of His chosen people the word of God brought the perfect law to make them holy and perfect to preserve their status as the chosen people of God. Moses received the law and as the spiritual leader of the children of Israel they embraced and preserved it for the future generation to ensure they will practice it so they will be blameless in the sight of God. The Mosaic law became the standard of God guiding not only His chosen people but also for every living souls that exists.

The Ten Commandments written by the hand of God was engraved in stone to make un-erasable and unchangeable. If we follow them then we become pleasing in His sight and there is no doubt we will gain His friendship and favor. The scribes and the Pharisees became its devoted practitioner fulfilling legalistically what God prescribed.

Indeed a clue was given to us why so many souls are lost because of our coldness and carelessness in following His commandments to perfection. Be holy and be perfect is what our Lord wants from us and this can only be done by fulfilling all the ten commandments to perfection. This is the kind of perfection that He wanted so we can become holy and perfect in His sight. And if the scribes and the Pharisees were expert in the law of God and they did practiced it and so must we. We must not only practice it to perfection but we must strive even higher than them so our soul will be save.

Our journey to our heavenly homeland is much much more difficult and demanding than what the children of Israel did in reaching the promised land. Bible scholars knew the great difficulties and extreme hardships encountered by Israel to the promised land. It is indeed just and right that we who aspires our greatest good must travel the most difficult and demanding road than Israel because the reward is much much more greater and desirable than the promised land.

In the promised land, they received material abundance filled with milk and honey. In the new covenant a new promise far beyond our limitless imagination where the reward is the possession of God and His kingdom where we share His beauty, majesty, splendor, power and glory. Paul, not finding the appropriate words to describe heaven simply said no ears heard nor eyes seen what is in store for those who loves Him. But as the reward is far beyond our expectation there is that challenging message from His mouth that we must also go beyond ourselves so we can completely possess God and heaven with the help of His grace and also with our own initiative and sincere effort making possible perfect union with God.

Therefore, do not be deceive by lying lips of false shepherds and teachers that it is easy to get to heaven by simply believing that Jesus did already paid our salvation with His death and all we have to do is to accept Him as Lord and Savior. To do so is good but there are conditions that must be done and that is to do the most holy will of God. As God did His part we too must do ours. Our journey to the new heaven is difficult as our Lord said.

"Enter ye in at the strait gate; for wide is the gate, and broad is the way that lead to destruction, and many there be which go thereat." (Matthew 7:13).

Our Lady's ministry kept on warning us that so many souls were lost to hell each day because we do not listen to our Lord who wants to see us all in heaven but our ears remained deaf and our hearts more hardened than ever before. We are more interested and more inspired in the promise land of this world which filled our mundane desires but destroyed the life of our immortal soul. There is no greater apostle and preacher than our Lady. She works unceasingly to made known how we can reached our greatest destination.

"Because strait is the gate, and narrow is the way which lead unto life, and few there be that find it" (Matthew 7:14).

This word came from our Lord's mouth certifying our Lady's warning that we have to really step up our spiritual life so to speak to be more holy and perfect than the Pharisees and not be deceived by so many lying lips that preached and taught the partiality of the truth, the way and the life. There are so many deceivers who is trying to win you using our Lord's name in vain risking many to lose their souls.

"Beware of false prophets, which comes to you in sheep's clothing, but inwardly they are ravening wolves." (Matthew 7:15).

Aware of the many enemies of our salvation, our Lady intensified her mission by calling and drawing faithful and devoted members of the Body of Christ to participate in teaching and preaching the fullness of God's truth for the salvation of souls. So very few realized nor recognized that the greatest missionary of God is none other than our Lady. She is not only Co-Redeemer but the hardest and the greatest laborer in our Lord's vineyard. After her death she received her glorious crown as queen of heaven and earth but she never rested on her deserved laurel with her constant apparition in so many places reminding her afflicted children to come and receive her as their own mother so she can intercede for them to Jesus knowing He would never refuse her.

Once again, our Lady's labor with her countless apparition were not taken seriously nor were appreciated by the ungrateful and the unbelievers. Her repeated messages for more prayers, penance, repentance and conversion were heard but so very few practiced it. And like her Son's teachings were preached and heard two thousand years ago still so few responded to the calling of holiness and perfection.

Such disregard for our eternal destiny, the Body of Christ weakened from the severity of its wounds and when the church that Christ established for our own greater good loses its life then the curtain of our existence will be lowered and darkness and death follows. And the Book of Life will finally be open and each one of us will know then where we will be.

Knowing this, our Lady sensing eternal death of her children and the condition of the church have called and instructed her little community to intensify their prayer life and to execute her Order to live the life of her Son to perfection by uniting oneself to the most Holy Trinity through her. Our Lady of Unity. By doing so, one will surely attain holiness and perfection with God's grace and through her powerful intercession. Thus, our Lady of Unity established her Order for the greatest glory and honor of the Triune God.

CHAPTER ONE

OUR ODYSSEY

It was in the garden of Eden that our story begins. What bitter sweet memory remembering how God and man were in constant contact never separated from each other until Adam and Eve were evicted from paradise. It was disobedience of God's single command that broke the closeness and it will take an extraordinary event to bring us back to such intimacy with the One who created us. The question then is when and where that extraordinary event will take place?

Sacred Scripture recorded the history of God and us and it was an ugly story and scene once our odyssey begins in a foreign land of our exile. Paradise was lost. We have lost everything that was all good and perfect by that single act of disobedience. It was a shocking change for Adam and Eve. There are no more handouts from God's generous bounty and in order for us to live and survive we have to labor strenuously even nights and days for our daily sustenance. The land of our exile was so shockingly different and strange for we are now subject to all that is not pleasant and agreeable to our senses. We now have to suffer all kinds of pains and afflictions never experienced before and most terrifying was losing our immortality and to face death. Worst than death was losing the great good God.

Once we lose God there is no longer light in our soul. Only darkness. We have lost His guidance and like a sheep without a shepherd we wandered aimlessly into the vast empty world not knowing the purpose of our existence. Losing God humanity became a hopeless and helpless being without a purpose or meaning and like a wounded disoriented beast we continued to live and behave like a beast concerned only for its own survival.

Thus, Cain killed his own brother much like the beast who kills for its own selfish instinct. Like an ugly wild beast, there is no more beauty in God's creation. We have lost the beauty of God made in His likeness. Once we lose Him our own free will took over dominated by the darkness of our soul and all our deeds were so unpleasant and horrific in God's eyes that He repented creating us. He was to destroy His creation but spared it when He found a man named Noah who shines in the midst of humanity's darkness and ugliness restraining Him not to end our existence. Noah's righteousness and goodness spared our destruction for God found something of a remnant of Himself. He found hope in Noah. Pleased with him, God preserved creation but the rest who were completely devoid of goodness were wiped out by the great flood.

A new generation from the family of Noah replenished the empty earth bringing new hope for His lofty purpose. Although humanity's struggle against the curses of sin continued to enslaved His people God also grant graces to chosen ones like Abraham who won His favor by his obedience to sacrifice the life of his one and only son and by doing so was rewarded being father of many nations. Abraham's blessings passed into Isaac and into Jacob, Isaac 's son and God as a preview of the future, came as one of us when He and Jacob wrestled.

"And Jacob was left alone; and there wrestled a man with him until the breaking of the day."

Jacob would not let him free unless he bless him. He asked Jacob his name and God changed it to Israel. What Jacob encountered was not man but God Himself in the flesh who made the first move so we will be made closer to Him. The new name of Israel was in a way a type of baptism of God's chosen people who will be His instrument of salvation for all His creation.

Thus Israel was blest with twelve sons but his youngest Joseph was sold by his jealous brothers to a merchant where he was taken as a slave to Egypt. By God's design and plan Joseph was raised up to the highest position in Egypt and when the great famine came the family of Israel were saved. Joseph was then reunited with his father and brothers in the land of Egypt where they enjoyed the abundances of the land. Thus, the tribe of Israel with God's providence multiplied rapidly in Egypt and as time passed by the memory of Joseph's great works in the past were quickly forgotten by the new ruler. Suspicious of Israel's tremendous growth in population and afraid they might turn against Egypt, Pharaoh issued an order that all new born babies be killed save the girls. Such order prompted a mother to hide her child in a basket and floated in into the river where an Egyptian princess found the child and by God's will the boy was saved and brought up to live with the Egyptian princess.

The boy was Moses destined to be the greatest prophet and as the story went he had to flee from Egypt for he had committed murder by killing an Egyptian. In his exile, while tending sheep Moses was drawn by the sight of a burning bush and he climbed to the mountain of Sinai and there he encountered the living God.

"And he said, drew not nigh hither; put off thy shoes from off thy feet whereon they standest is holy ground." (Exodus 3:5).

It was a calling designed for Moses so we His people will know that God truly exist and is always present in our lives and activities. It was the beginning in fulfilling God's perfect plan to make us His greatest work-our perfection. By the fall of our first parents we were evicted from paradise and separated from God. Without God we wandered aimlessly in life striving only to live and survive in a new environment that is undesirable and unpleasant. It was the most difficult time for us to be without God's friendship and sin became the way of life uncontrollable that God destroyed it in the great flood save Noah and his family.

From the line of Noah God raise Moses to be His greatest prophet in that time. It was on Mount Sinai that God commissioned Moses to free His chosen people from slavery finally answering the prayers and the cries of Israel's children.

"And the Lord said, I have surely seen the affliction of my people which are in Egypt, and have heard their cry by reason of their taskmasters for I know their sorrows." (Exodus 3:7).

And to shortened the story Moses lead Israel into freedom after so many difficult encounter and confrontation with Pharaoh. It was on this many confrontations that the Almighty God showed His awesome power. First, by turning Aaron's rod into a serpent. Second, by changing the river water into blood. Thirdly, frogs flooded the land of Egypt. Fourthly, changing dust into lice infecting both man and beast. Fifthly, God sent swarms of flies into the houses of the Egyptian. Sixthly, God smote all of Egypt's livestock but spared what belongs to Israel. Seventhly, all Egyptians were afflicted with boils. Eighthly, God sent hail and mingled with fire and thunder over the Egyptians destroying herbs and fruit trees. Ninthly, God covered the land with locusts filling Egypt's land and houses. Tenthly, God covered the land in total darkness for three days but Pharaoh would not let God's people go. Evidently, God has its own limits and He had to execute the final act.

"And the Lord said unto Moses, yet I will bring one plaque more upon Pharaoh and upon Egypt; afterwards he will let you go hence; when he shall let you go he shall surely thrust you out hence altogether." (Exodus 11:1).

Thus, God struck all first born Egyptian both man and beast including all the gods of Egypt dead. These events were recorded and verified in the history of Egypt witnessed both by the Jewish and Egyptian people revealing God's mighty power.

Once freed the people of Israel begin their journey to the promised land but Pharaoh came to his senses and decided to renege on his promise realizing the slaves will be Egypt's great loss. Pharaoh gathered his army to chase them. By doing so, God showed Israel and Egypt the greatest miracle mankind will ever saw by the parting of the Red Sea creating a path of dry land so His people can walked through. Pharaoh's army chased and followed them but God blocked their path with a pillar of fire and took off their chariot wheels disabling their pursuit.

"And the waters returned, and covered the chariots and the horsemen, and all the host of Pharaoh that came into the sea after them; there remained not so much as one of them." (Exodus 14:28).

What they saw made Israel's faith strongest having seen the great works of their God. Indeed, God was their helper and deliverer. He destroyed Egypt's mighty army.

"Pharaoh's chariots and his host he cast into the sea; his chosen captains also are drowned in the Red Sea." (Exodus 15:4).

Thus the song of Moses echoed even to our generation who are so blest to hear how great and good really God is.

"Who is like unto thee, O Lord, among the gods? Who is like thee, glorious in holiness, fearful in praises doing wonders." (Exodus 15:11).

By sharing their experiences with the real and living God the whole world are bless for we have received from them that God wants to be known, loved and to be served.

Free at last, they were anxious and excited to begin their odyssey to the promised land with Moses leading the way.

"So Moses brought Israel from the Red Sea, and they went into the wilderness of Shur; and they went three days in the wilderness, and found no water." (Exodus 15;22). There is nothing worst than traveling in the desert and Israel suffered much in the heat of the day and the cold at night. Dehydration is the greatest culprit and once the body is deprived of water it could die. When the body lacked water it will suffer all kinds of ailment and will weakened the strongest of men. Thus, their strong faith in Moses started to erode.

"And the people murmured against Moses, what shall we drink?" (Exodus 15:24).

Nothing much has changed for us. The burden of our flesh simply weakened our spirit. It is our daily struggle by always complaining even though we have all the comfort and conveniences technology had brought us. But what Israel suffered in their odyssey was much worse than ours.

God heard Moses's intercession and He showed him the tree if casted into the water of Marah sweet. Thus, by this miracle God made a statute and ordinance for His people.

"And said, if thou diligently hearken to the voice of the Lord thy God, and wilt do that which is right in his sight, and wilt give ear to his commandments and keep all his statutes, I will put none of these diseases upon thee, which I have brought upon the Egyptians: for I am the Lord that healed thee." (Exodus 15:26).

Clearly, it is always in obedience that God is pleased. Obviously, when He is pleased God will always protect and provides the obedient one. Initially, God's chosen people were obedient but became chronic complainer and even went further by blaming Him in their little inconveniences.

"And the children of Israel said unto them would to God we had died by the hand of the Lord in the land of Egypt when we sat by the flesh pots and when we did eat bread to the full; for ye have brought us forth unto this wilderness, to kill this assembly with hunger." (Exodus 16:3).

God's love and mercy prevailed despite His displeasure by providing them abundant bread in the morning and quails for their meat in the evening. They keep on their journey but when there was no water in the place of Massah and Meribath the Lord was even more gracious by providing them their needs.

Reaching Mount Sinai, Moses went up to received God's commandments but once he was gone for forty days and nights the tribe of Israel became restless and anxious thinking Moses dead. Once again, our rebellious nature offended God when they fashioned a golden calf and offered burnt offerings to their newly found god. They were celebrating wildly by eating, drinking and playing that they became abominable in God's sight.

"And the Lord said unto Moses, Go, get thee down; for thy people, which thou brought out of the land of Egypt, have corrupted themselves." (Exodus 33:7).

In his anger Moses threw the two tablets at their feasting and broke it. In His just anger the idolaters were slain.

"And the Lord plaque the people because they made the calf which Aaron made." (Exodus 32:35).

Once the dust settled the chosen people of God did received the Ten Commandments. All of God's commands if obeyed perfectly will eventually restore the beauty of his image in our soul. For the just and the righteous His commandments are not a burden but for the wicked and rebellious impossible to follow.

The exodus of God's chosen people were nothing else but a preview that all of us must make our own odyssey where all kinds of trials and tribulations are to be expected. No doubt, it will be difficult for us all. Even Moses the chosen one considered the greatest prophet of Israel could not make it to God's promise land.

"And the Lord said unto him, this is the land I sworn unto Abraham, unto Isaac and unto Jacob, saying I will give it unto thy seed; I have caused thee to see it with thine eyes but thou shalt not go over thither." (Exodus 34:4).

Israel's journey to their promised land make us think seriously that our odyssey to the new heavens is far more demanding and challenging. Justly so, for our rewards is not corporal, is not worldly honor, treasure, pleasure or wealth but the greatest reward is none other than God. Knowing this, our Lady of Unity will be persistent in her apostolic mission in trying to lure everyone to come to her so she will be the second intercessor for our salvation.

Help me help you. Come to me and take me as your own mother.

REFLECTION:

"In journeyings often, in perils of waters, in perils of robbers, in perils by mine own countrymen, in perils by the heathen, in perils in the city, in perils in the wilderness, in perils in the sea, in perils among false brethren;" (2 Corinthians 11:26).

If God's chosen apostle experienced such severe sufferings in his mission so must we who aspire to reach our destination. And if the children of Israel went through such severe trials and tribulations for their promised land, we should meditate with our own odyssey that it will not be that easy and not to be deceived by false shepherds that all we have to do was to believe that Jesus is Lord and Savior. Such gospel is devilish risking many souls to eternal death. The truth is our journey to the new heaven and to become like God is not accomplished by merely believing and accepting Jesus as Lord and God. If it cost so much pain, sufferings, trials and even death in possessing the promised land it will obviously costs us much much more in getting the reward of heaven and God.

This is our Lady's pleading to all God's people to let her help them so we can possess the greatest imaginable reward we can ever long or hope for.

PRAYER:

Hail, Holy Queen, mother of mercy, our life, our sweetness and our hope. To thee do we cry, poor banished children of Eve. To thee we send up our sighs mourning and weeping in this valley of tears. Turn then, most gracious advocate, thine eyes of mercy toward us. And after this our exile, show unto us the blessed fruit of thy womb, Jesus, O clement, O loving sweet Virgin Mary.

Pray for us, O holy mother of God.

That we may be made worthy of the promises of Christ.

This prayer to our Lady will not go in vain.

CHAPTER TWO
· ·
HIS ODYSSEY

Fulfilling His promise the tribe of Israel finally possessed their promised land and they celebrated by paying homage to their God. Forty long years wandering in the desert. They survived because God never abandoned them despite their despicable and displeasing behavior. Now, they have freedom and with their own fertile land where they can abundantly produce crops and vegetables. They became prosperous but as time passed by they have wandered away from their God.

"Hear, O heavens, and give ear O earth; for the Lord hath spoken, I have nourished and brought up children and they have rebelled against me." (Isaiah 1:2).

Since the fall, the curses of sin is in our blood and it has been our nature and tendency to commit sin. Thus, what God commanded for our highest good was in conflict of what we desire as our own highest good. Such contradicting ideology damages our relationship with God destroying once again His works restoring the beauty of our being.

"Ah sinful nation, a people laden with iniquity a seed of evil doers children that are corrupters; they have forsaken the Lord they have provoked the Holy One of Israel into anger they are gone away backward." (Isaiah 1:4).

Indeed, we are hopeless and helpless sinner!!! From the fall of our first parents every generation could not stop sinning. How could we do all of these to the great good God who had done everything for our greatest good? He had blest us abundantly and never stop loving and caring for us. Why can we not stop sinning?

The prophet Isaiah's admonition to the tribe of Israel can now be extended to our own time. Since our fall, there is no remedy for sin. Despite God's blessings, goodness and kindness is never enough to draw us to Him.

"Ah her people sigh, the seek bread; they have given their pleasant things for meat to relieve the soul; see O Lord, and consider; for I am vile."

Such was, is and will be the greatest burden of our soul struggling unable to conquer our sinfulness. There is no remedy for our vileness and wickedness and there is no hope for us. Knowing our condition God must make His own odyssey to heal the sickness of our soul by lowering Himself from the highest heaven to the lowest place in the land of our exile. His odyssey will transform God into man and man into God.

"Therefore the Lord Himself shall give you a sign; Behold a virgin shall conceive, and bear a son, and shall call his name Immanuel." (Isaiah 7:14).

All waited for a long time the coming of the Messiah who will come to be with us fulfilling the prophecy of Isaiah. But before His coming came the greatest prophet of the new covenant.

"There was a man sent from God, whose name was John." (St John 1:6).

Isaiah prophesied the name Immanuel which meant God with us and the prophet of the new covenant echoed Isaiah's prophecy.

"And the word was made flesh and dwell among us." (St John 1:14).

Thus the greatest promise did came and God became man in the Persona of Christ Jesus the long awaited savior. Jesus Christ is known to the whole world as the Messiah. He is God and man revered and accepted by Christians and other religion also knew and heard his name. Christians acknowledged that Jesus was born of the virgin Mary conceived by the Holy Spirit. He spent time preaching and teaching the way, the truth and the life and anyone who believes in Him will have eternal life. He chose twelve disciples to be His companion in spreading the Gospel so the world will know that He had come. They have witnessed all His miracles and also saw their Savior cruelly condemned and crucified on the cross. Scared, His chosen followers fled from the scene knowing that they too will suffer the same fate if they professed their faith as His disciples. As they were mostly ignorant and uneducated fishermen saved a few the Christian religion should have also died with Jesus death on the cross.

Destroy the temple and on the third day I will rebuilt it. Jesus followers had no idea about what He told them that on the third day He will rise from the dead.

Afraid and desperate of what will become of them Jesus disciples remained in hiding and when Mary Magdalene told them she had seen the risen Lord, they believed not. Until He appeared to them. And when Thomas was told about Jesus resurrection he too was a doubter. But once Thomas saw Him and touched His wounds he fell on his knees and proclaimed, "My Lord and my God."

The rising of Jesus from the dead became a historic hysteria drawing many to follow Him. The timid disciples were radically changed into fearless followers proclaiming their risen Lord. Everyone was excited to hear them preached and quickly became believers and converted to the faith. Indeed, the world was changed dramatically where this new and dynamic religion give humanity the greatest and brightest hope for our salvation.

As many more followers saw the risen Lord living among them the Christian faith spread rapidly converting many to this incredible religion where the Word made flesh became a reality and a part of human history. The extraordinary event had come.

Alleluia, the Lord has risen. The Messiah had come and salvation is here!!! This is the Christian's voice echoing all over the world during Easter a grand celebration of how the resurrection of our Lord became our hope. That we, too will be risen from the dead and follow His ascension to heaven there we will join our Head rejoicing for the reward of His promises.

As the result of His coming the world did changed and the Christian faith became the beacon of light that brings hope to our hopeless condition. The extraordinary event restored us back to Him. Most important, God's coming into the world not only accomplished our redemption but also the establishment of his much needed church so believers can be integrated into his mystical Body so the enemies of God can never destroy His church thus preserving His works of our redemption, sanctification and salvation. The church with all its sacraments can never be destroyed.

"And I say unto thee that thou art Peter and upon this rock I will build my church and the gates of hell shall not prevail against it." (Matthew 16:18).

The arrival of Christ in our midst change the complexion of the earth. The old earth had passed away. Now, in the new earth, the foundation of Christ and the building of His Body composed of baptized believers and sustained by its powerful sacraments became the standard of God's real Presence in the world. Now and until the end of time God will remain with us helping and guiding us to the new heavens.

Powered by God's presence, thousands of churches were built all over the world as millions of believers were baptized and became member of his Body. Together on Sundays, they attended Holy Mass celebrating the Paschal mystery giving thanks and praises to God. Before its tremendous growth, the first Christian church decided to build a hierarchy to maintain order, unity and stability with Peter chosen as its leader. Thus, the Papacy or the Chair of Peter as its spiritual leader became a well-oiled church organization with billions of followers around the world. The church of Saint Peter in Rome has become the symbol of Christianity of which believers looked up to him. However, Martin Luther revolted of the church's ways of raising funds by selling indulgences and many followed him. And so the Christian faith were splintered with all kinds of Christian churches but despite its division Jesus Christ was and is still the center of Christian worship.

Despite the billions of Christian followers, Christ redemptive works had barely scratch the surface of our salvation since billions or more practiced and embraced other religion where Christ is not accepted as the Messiah. The Islam, Hindu, Buddhist and the Jewish religion had billions of their own followers and they do not believe nor accept Him as God and man. They only believe in God and that Jesus Christ is not. And so the world remained greatly divided not only morally but culturally but also in their religion. Such division did create some serious problems that even lead to violence and death.

Although the division remains, the world we live in now was a much better place because it owed to the Jewish people chosen by God to be the bearer of His Words. The world should be grateful to them for sharing the real and living God. Without God, the world would have been destroyed long ago like the days of Noah when God did not exist in their midst. He existed but they do not want God.

The revelation of God to His chosen people inspired many to seek and know Him. The Jewish religion shared to the world the Old and New Testament teaching and showing us how we can possess the kingdom of

God and with the promise to live in eternal happiness in the new heaven. God not only revealed Himself and His kingdom but also of His coming to our world for our redemption and salvation so we can be united with Him.

Thus the world became the battleground between believers and unbelievers. Despite God's revelation there still exist unbelievers who condemned religion as an escape providing false hope that there is nothing more after our life ends. This ongoing battle will continue but believers never lose hope that God'e revelation is the absolute truth.

"Him that over cometh will I make a pillar in the temple of my God and he shall go no more out; and I will write upon him the name of the city of God, which is new Jerusalem, which cometh down of heaven from my God; and I will write upon him my new name." (Revelation 3:12).

This is the word of God and to believers who persevere will surely reap the promised reward. And God will crowned them as heirs and sharers of His kingdom.

"Behold, I come quickly, hold that fast which thou hast, that no man take thy crown." (Revelation 3:11).

God reminds us of the difficult battle against the world, the devil and flesh but encourages us never to give up nor surrender against our enemies for His reward is more than worth it.

"To him that over cometh will I grant to sit with me in my throne even as I also overcame, and am set down with my Father in His throne." (Revelation 3:21).

How could anybody refuse such offer? We labored so strenuously for worthless and unnecessary things that brings nothing but pains and sufferings while the promise of God is truly real. Such promise should enflame our hearts and soul to give our all to Him. To the unbelievers and obstinate sinners if they persisted in rebelling against God their judgement will be worse than death.

"And the kings of the earth, and the great men, and the rich men, and the chief captains, and the mighty men, and every bondman, and every freeman, hid themselves in the dens and in the rocks of the mountain."

The Book of Revelation's warning is now and for eternity and the dreaded day of reckoning is not a thousand years away but it is for those who will die this moment as Our Lady of Unity persistently revealed that each single day thousands and thousands were lost because of their obstinate rejection of her Son. She keeps pleading and pleading to the

Triune God and to specially to us for she knew the eternal agony to those who were lost in hell.

"And said to the mountains and rocks, fall on us, and hide us from the face of Him that sit on the throne, and from the wrath of the Lamb; For the great day of His wrath is come; and who shall be able to stand?" (Revelation 6:16-17).

Before God's revelation comes into reality we have the greatest chance of saving our soul by accepting and embracing what Jesus and His church taught and not to reject the fullness of truth. As He made an odyssey into our forsaken world, let us embrace and welcome Him and do everything by becoming true followers of the God man. Above all, let us truly love Him not by words but by our works and the complete giving of our lives to Him.

REFLECTION:

"Though He was in the form of God, Jesus did not deem equality with God something to be grasped at. Rather, He emptied Himself and took the form of a slave, being born in the likeness of men. He was known to be of human estate, and it was thus that he humbled Himself, obediently accepting even death, death on the cross. Because of this, God highly exalted Him and bestowed on Him the name above every other name so that at Jesus, name every knee must bend in the heavens, on the earth, and under the earth, And every tongue proclaim to the glory of God the Father. Jesus Christ is Lord!"

He made His odyssey. What grave injustice done to our God if we continue our ingrate behavior in refusing to acknowledge and to believe that everything He did was for our greatest and highest good. From His glorious throne in heaven the King of angels the Lord of all changed Himself into like us. He was immortal and became mortal so He would taste the horrifying and terrifying moment of death. Like Adam and Eve who suffered the sting of death so did our Almighty God to show us that death has no longer power over us for He did conquered it. Jesus who is sinless joined us in the land of our exile so He can become the perfect sacrifice and offering to the Father so justice and peace became the avenue that would bring us back to God. Because of the hopelessness and helplessness of our situation God alone must get involved in gathering

13

and drawing us back but it did cost Him so much. By losing His life we gain more than heaven for we have received God.

From our hopeless and helpless condition spring our greatest gift and that is our second chance to live that glorious life of God.

Yes, God emptied Himself completely and even took the form of a slave to show us how much He truly loves us and the price of our ransom should made us forever indebted to Him. What He wants from us was simply to follow Him so Jesus our Lord will take and bring us back to where we belong. To ignore and deny what Jesus did for us is indeed the greatest injustices done to the great and good God and being perfectly just, judgement cannot be denied. If the angels in heaven bent their knees in Jesus name so all of us here on earth must likewise do. God's odyssey must be remembered, revered, pondered, honored, treasured and to embraced it with our greatest love.

PRAYER:

O Mother of all peoples; you know all their sufferings and their hopes. You maternally feel all their struggles between good and evil, between the light and the darkness which shake the world. Receive our cry, directed to the Holy Spirit straight to your heart and, with the love of the Mother and Handmaid of the Lord, embrace the individuals and peoples who must look for this embrace, together with the individuals and peoples to those you attend in a particular way. Take the entire human family under your maternal protection. With outflows of affection, O Mother, we entrust it to you. May the time of peace and liberty approach for all, the time of truth, justice and hope. Our Lady of Unity pray for us sinners now and at the hour of death. Amen.

CHAPTER THREE
. . . .
OUR CALLING

"Then the Lord rained upon Sodom and upon Gomorrah brimstone and fire from the Lord out of heaven." (*Genesis 19:24).

Never should we abused the goodness of God nor forget His justice will swiftly shift the scale to an irrevocable sentence to those who keeps provoking Him to anger. God's wrath is a terrifying thing to see. We are shocked when a big earthquake swallowed buildings and houses killing hundreds of thousand and wondered if the world is near its end. Once the tragic event passed we go on with our lives and forgetting those terrible tragic events. Then, the world was shocked when the mighty twin towers in New York crumbled into ashes killing thousands inflicting terror and concern of the security and safety of the world's greatest nation. Churches were filled fearful what will happen next. Then, again as time passed churches became empty as fear had subsided. Pastor keep preaching to its flock that all those tragic events that kept on happening is a part of God's judgement reminding us that death is like a shadow following each one of us and that we should be always prepared for our own judgement. God is always calling us but do we hear Him?

"And the Lord said, because the city of Sodom and Gomorrah is great, and because their sin is very great."(Genesis 18:20).

Like what is happening in our time Sodom and Gomorrah was filled with wickedness and evil. Fornication, adultery and homosexuality were so rampant that even the visiting angels in Lot's house were not spared with their lustfulness. Such wanton wickedness God could no longer tolerate. God had no choice but to destroy His creation, like He did in Noah's time.

"And the flood was forty days upon the earth; and the waters increased, and bare up the ark, and it was lift up above the earth." (Genesis 7:18).

It is always our sin and our unwillingness to repent and change driving God to wrath.

"And the Lord said to Noah, Come thou and all thy house into the ark; for thee have I seen righteous before me in this generation." (Genesis 7:1).

It is the righteous and the just that can appease the rage of God. The heart of God is full of love, mercy and kindness. And His patience is way beyond our understanding. He will try to keep control of His rage and anger as long as He can but there comes that time when all our sin can no longer be tolerated. We should note that had God found just one righteous soul like Noah, Sodom and Gomorrah would have been spared.

"And He said, Oh let not the Lord be angry, and I will speak yet but his once; peradventure ten shall be found there. And He said, I will not destroy it for ten's sake."

None was found even one in Sodom and Gomorrah that fits God's saving standard. But on the new earth aside from our Lord, there is someone so special who can easily appease the wrath of God. She is none other but God's daughter, mother and spouse.

Our Lady's appearance did made the greatest difference in consoling and controlling God's wrath. She appeared at Fatima in 1917 knowing the world's wickedness was out of control and she must intervened and the world was spared. Had she not appeared at Fatima the world would have ended. She appeared to the three little lamb and they willingly answered the call to prayer, fasting, penance for the conversion of the world. These three little innocent children offered themselves by living a simple life of prayer and penance and they were so fruitful. Unlike Sodom and Gomorrah, deprived of our Lord's real presence and without our Lady's powerful intercession and with no responder to the calling of conversion, God had no choice but to destroy the city infested with sin. Even the pleading of Abraham, His chosen one, could not change the heart of God. Abraham's righteousness was not enough.

Mary knew she is much needed in our world for she was specially chosen to possessed and dispensed the fullness of God's grace so she can be an active participant in completing His greatest works. Our Lady is needed by God's First Persona, her eternal Father to be His ark, by God's Second Persona so in her womb the birth of God and man becomes a reality to consummate the unity of divinity and humanity. Mary is truly needed by God's Third Persona to be His spouse so our Lady will receive God's genetic seed to form the long awaited Immanuel. Although Joseph was Mary's husband, the camouflaged marriage was to cover the Messiah's coming. Mary was only wedded to the Third Persona of God, the Holy Spirit for it was divinely ordained and not to compromised her stature. Mary's purity and immaculacy was always preserved in time and eternity and no man including Joseph can touch her.

"Then said Mary unto the angel how shall this be, seeing I know not a man?" (Luke 1:34).

Mary's inner desire was honored by the most High God and it was His ordaining will that she had nothing to do with Joseph in terms of physical and sexual union. Both were chosen playing their worldly role in accordance to the perfect plan of God. Joseph was a pure chase man specially chosen by God to be Mary's guardian in preserving the immaculacy and purity of God's chosen spouse. God knew Joseph and he was the perfect choice not only to guard and preserve Mary's divine dignity but also to be the foster father of His only begotten Son.

Of course, came disagreement from Christian churches who could not accept Mary's virginity and purity. They argued that Mary was pure and immaculate when she encountered the archangel Gabriel proclaiming that she was specially chosen to bear God's only begotten Son but after the birth of Jesus they claimed that Mary and Joseph entered into a relationship that produced children of their own.

"Then came then his brethren and his mother, and, standing without, sent unto him, calling him." (Mark 4:31).

With their own interpretation of the Gospel, they concluded that Jesus indeed had brothers children of both Mary and Joseph. However, Holy Mother Church simply ignored them knowing of the deficiency in their teachings. The Catholic Church with the approval of the See of Peter did proclaimed the dogma of Mary's immaculacy and that she was and is free from any stain of sin. And the dogma was certified by the appearance of our Lady to Bernadette at Lourdes. Such gross error showed how other Christian churches marginalized Mary's role and they even lowered her divine dignity into the level of our baseness.

"I am the Immaculate Conception." She proclaimed the church's dogma as truth.

But all arguments or disagreements is really irrelevant for what is of great importance is how we promptly respond to this glorious calling of God. Procrastination deceives many to lose their immortal souls. Our Lady revealed to the three children at Fatima that thousands and thousands of souls were lost to hell because of such attitude. They have forgotten that time belongs to God and to misuse it will be our greatest loss. She warned.

"Therefore be ye also ready: for in such an hour ye think not the Son of man cometh." (Matthew 24:44).

Our Lady is calling us her children not to wait for tomorrow but to promptly obey her Son's warning. We have to be vigilant now for death comes in an unexpected moment taking away our only chance of salvation.

"Watch therefore; for ye know not your Lord doth come." (Matthew 24:42).

This is our greatest mistake why so many souls were lost to hell. Procrastination. We have been greatly deceived that death will not come to us since we are young, strong and healthy but the obituaries contradicts such assumption. In fact, hundreds of thousands dies every day. Are we exempt? Death is our destination. The truth is once we are born we begin to inch closer to the grave. For this reason, Our Lady keep on working calling her children for conversion. Our Lady's call is now echoing her Son's teaching that the time of our salvation is now. Not tomorrow. There is a tomorrow but no guarantee that we will see it.

Our Lady's great love for her children is simply like our Lord's love for us. Every time a single soul is lost the pain and suffering she endured seeing Jesus died on the cross brought the same torment. Out of gratitude to our Triune God let us give some respect and appreciation to the mother of our Savior by answering her call of conversion. Doing what our mother calls us to do makes us a brother or a sister to her Son, Jesus. Our conversion will bring us back to live the life of God and we will have the joy of our salvation.

"For this my Son was dead and is alive again; he was lost and is found. And they began to be merry." (Luke 15:23).

Our conversion to God is the only way we can avoid eternal death. We are dead to sin but repentance brought us back alive to God. Once converted the life of God through the Holy Spirit starts transforming and restoring the soul into the likeness of His Being. Once ugly now beautiful. This is our calling, restoring the beauty of God by making His Life our very own.

REFLECTION:

"I press toward the mark for the prize of the high calling of God in Christ Jesus." (Philippians 3:14).

Do not ignore the calling of God because once your ears heard His voice and you never listen to His Words darkness will be your constant companion. Blindness follows deafness and godlessness becomes the banner of the soul. Once God is out of the equation one is definitely destines to eternal destruction. Our calling is not a pipe dream nor a fantasy but truly reality. In our deafness and blindness is that tendency to ignore God's calling thereby missing the mark and dismissing His prize as nothing of value. Most of us chose to answer the calling of the world. Once God's calling is ignored we declared war against Him and such sad situation will definitely our greatest loss. Once God became our enemy what chance do we have? Therefore, consider what God had prepared for you. Consider what He had to undergo for you? Can you just sit silently and ponder and think seriously what awaits to those who chose to love and serve Him.

PRAYER:

Hail holy Mary, Mother of God who promptly answered the calling of the Triune God without any hesitation do pray for us your afflicted children blinded and deceived by the enemies of our salvation, obtain for us the grace of true conversion that we too like you will answer quickly His calling to be holy and perfect so we may gain our salvation. Our Lady of Unity, pray for us sinners now and at the moment of our judgement. Amen.

CHAPTER FOUR

. . . .

THE GREATEST CALLING

"And the angel came in unto her, and said, Hail thou art highly favored, the Lord is with thee: blessed art thou among women." (Luke 1:28).

In our history, the calling of Mary was the greatest. The lowly maiden was engaged to Joseph for marriage and both were destined in executing God's work transforming dust into divinity.

Adam was called as steward of God's garden commanded to guard the tree of life. He had everything and it was truly paradise we all seek and work hard to possess it. And to make him happy, God gave Eve as his wife and companion. It would have been better though for Adam to be alone for Eve tempted Adam to disobey God by eating the fruit of the forbidden tree. By doing so, Adam failed God in his calling.

Like Adam and Eve, we too, are destined to fail God from His highest calling of holiness. Receiving His curse, we became helpless and hopeless wandering not knowing the purpose of our existence. Until the angel appeared to Mary announcing the greatness of her calling but trusted not the messenger.

"And when she saw him, she was troubled at his saying and cast in her mind what manner of salutation this should be."

Even before the angel told her, God had already bestowed on Mary the fullness of grace. It was the grace of perfect humility that Mary questioned how could she be highly favored by God when she considered herself a very lowly handmaid. With the grace of discernment she acted prudently and wisely by simply waiting what will be the purpose of the message.

Eve on the other hand promptly took the fruit of the tree without any hesitation upon hearing the voice of the serpent that they become like

God once the fruit was eaten. In our own calling let us imitate our Lady's response by carefully and thoughtfully assessing the situation we are in. It is always wise to pray, to deliberate and to wait.

"And the angel said unto her, Fear not, Mary; for thou hast found favor with God." (Luke 1:30).

We are not like Mary for God had predestined her to be His perfect model for us. But do not be down casted nor be dismayed for we too are highly favored by God because Mary was chosen and ordained for our own sake so we can have the fruits of her blessed womb. Indeed, we too are highly favored because like her God created us for Himself. All we have to do is to make the greatest effort in knowing, loving and serving Him. Once we do that, like Mary, we will have the greatest chance to earned that glorious crown reserved to those who love the One who created us. If we imitate our Lord's and our Lady's life then we are certain to gain heaven.

"And behold, thou shalt conceive in thy womb, and bring forth a son, and shalt call his name Jesus." (Luke 1:31).

The presence of Gabriel, the archangel did not intimidate her, even suspicious of his message knowing that she is a virgin. Mary was distrustful of what she heard even if it came from an angel.

"And the angel answered and said unto her, the Holy Ghost shall come upon thee and the power of the Highest shall overshadow thee; therefore, also that holy thing which shall be born of thee shall be called Son of God." (Luke 1:35).

The mention of the birth of the Messiah enlightened Mary that the message was true for it has been prophesied that He will be born through a virgin birth and this God child will be conceived by the Holy Spirit. She was humbled realizing such calling was the greatest and as an obedient daughter of God she made her yes. Mary knew that her Father in heaven had prepared her for a very special mission and once she heard the message she was ready and willing. God the Father chose a very simple and humble maiden and God ordained that His chosen daughter will be free from the stain of original sin. Although all of Adam's offsprings was cursed with sin, Mary was exempted from it. Such divine design made Mary as the only creature without any sin so her virginal womb will be the perfect place where divinity and humanity merged. The most holy God will never dwell in a house of sin nor He will be conceive on a woman stained with sin. Knowing sin as God's greatest enemy, Mary must be free and clear of any speck of sin.

21

Logically, if Mary was conceived with original sin, then there is no way salvation is possible. The only way to accomplish God's plan for our redemption, sanctification and salvation was to make Mary like Jesus.

Mary must also be pure, perfect and holy for she will become the spouse of the Holy Spirit. As the spouse of God, Mary's immaculacy is essential and so necessary in order to fulfill God's plan so Jesus will be conceived free and clear of any stain or speck of sin. It is not possible that the Holy Spirit will chose a spouse stained with sin. Most could never understand the church dogma that Mary, the mother of Jesus was the immaculate one. The world covered in darkness remains blinded. They will never recognize nor realize that Mary is the mother of salvation and co redeemer and she was conceived without sin.

Thus, our Lady appeared before a very simple uneducated maiden Bernadette at Lourdes, France to validate and confirm the church dogma that indeed she was pure and perfect. Bernadette, uneducated as she was had no idea that it was Mary who appeared to her and like an innocent child she obeyed her instruction to pray the rosary. On her next encounter, not knowing she was the Blessed Virgin Mary, she asked her name and Mary replied that she was the Immaculate Conception. Bernadette had no clue what it meant.

Endless argument however will go on about Mary's immaculacy since biblical scholars and theologians have universally accepted that we are all sinners and only Jesus is sinless. However, Mary received the fullness of God's graces which included her redemption, sanctification and salvation. As His only beloved daughter, God the Father freely and fully bestowed on her all of that is His, including the gift of her immaculacy. Like her Father, Mary inherited His All. If God's singular grace suffices for the salvation of humanity think about the fullness of God's grace. We are thinking about the greatness of Mary's gift. Before Mary was even conceived in her mother's womb God had already planned the she will be the recipient of His greatest gift bestowed on any creature.

There is no need of Mary to be redeemed, sanctified and saved for the Triune God had made an exception since she will be a major participant in the economy of our salvation. She had to enter into the divine drama where she is the morning star shining brightly giving humanity hope from the darkness of its exile. Like a loving mother, she will feed us her hungry children, the Bread of life and from her immaculate breast flowed the milk of God's graces nourishing and nurturing us until we are weaned into the likeness of her divine Son. We owed Mary some reverence and respect not only because she is the mother of God but also the mother of salvation. She is the mother of all souls. Wither one is a Catholic, Methodist, Jewish, Muslim, Hindu or whatever religion, Mary was ordained to be our mother and by honoring her, we in no way offended or dishonored the Triune God. On the contrary, when we honor and revere Mary, we tripled the honor and glory of God.

How so?

Our heavenly Father will be pleased to see His beloved daughter is honored and revered. Would not any father be greatly honored and pleased if his daughter received one? Certainly, it will always touch the heart of our heavenly Father seeing us honoring the Blessed Virgin Mary. The Catholic Church will always venerate and honor Mary as Mother of God and with her protection the power of hell will not prevail. Come to think of it that the United States of America made Mary as its patroness and protectress through the consecrated action of the Catholic Church and God indeed had blest America with material abundance and immense wealth. Like the Catholic Church, America will always be protected and preserved because of our Lady's intercession. Those who rejected or ignored her will suffer the greatest loss simply because she had all of God's graces readily available for dispensing to anyone who called on her. Millions had testified how the Blessed Virgin Mary helped them with their needs, corporal or spiritual.

Christ Jesus, the only begotten Son of the Father will be greatly pleased and glorified if one honored and revered His beloved mother. He even inspired the church to honor Mary a co redeemer which made her seemingly equal to Jesus in the works of our salvation. Of course, many will cry heresy knowing that only Jesus can save our soul. Such notion that Mary is co redeemer will create chaos and controversy for it is only God in His Second Persona who can redeem, restore and save our soul. To think or say otherwise is heretical. What was written in Sacred Scriptures are truth and anyone who disagree about the saving of work of Jesus will have the greatest difficulty in proclaiming that there is a co redeemer.

But, in mystical theology, Mary's title as co redeemer has validity although billions will not agree. Jesus alone is the most worthy to do the redeeming and saving plans of God but Mary is also deserving of the title co redeemer even though a creature like us except sin. As the mother of our Redeemer and Savior she was and always be united with Jesus laboring for the salvation of mankind. Listen to our Lord.

"Mother behold thy Son."

Mary understood the hidden meaning of His Words. Jesus knew that we are and always be problematic in taking great care for our eternal destiny and there is always that great shortage of laborer in His vineyard and He knew Mary was ordained by the Triune God as treasurer and dispenser of their graces.

She is not highly regarded as her Son since Mary is simply a lowly creature and should not be put on the divine pedestal. But if Jesus was ordained to save us then it was Mary's yes that made possible of her Son's entrance of His messianic mission.

As the chosen spouse of the Holy Spirit, Mary had access to all about her God. Of all God's creature Mary alone knew all God's secrets of which we all are deprived of. She is the mother of theologians for she alone fathoms the deepest mystery of the Triune God. As confusing and unfathomable was the concept of the Trinity, she alone understood clearly why this One Almighty God had to make Himself Three.

"Hail Mary full of grace the Lord is with you."

Over and over she was and is exalted and revered by the Catholic faithful for her powerful role in the salvation of mankind. And she was and is always united to the Triune God and Mary formed a community known as Our Lady of Unity where its greatest mission was to unite all His creation to the Blessed Trinity.

REFLECTION:

"And the angel answered and said unto her, the Holy Ghost shall come upon thee and the power of the Highest shall overshadow thee, therefore, also that holy thing which shall be born to thee shall be called Son of God." (Luke 1:35).

Adam and Eve were called to be steward of the garden of Eden, They totally failed God and we inherited the fruits of sin and death. Noah was called to gather God's creation into the ark to replenish the earth and his success brought a new generation that produced Abraham chosen to be father of many nations. Isaac, Abraham's son inherited God's blessing and Jacob was chosen to be the father of the twelve tribes of God's chosen people. Then Moses was called to lead Israel to freedom after their long years of slavery in Egypt.

In every time and period of the tribe of Israel came many distinguish and prominent servants and prophets of God and they responded well to their calling. David, Solomon, Isaiah, Jeremiah were chosen by God according to His purpose and plan. But the greatest calling was Mary for she will become the mother of God. She was the greatest of all God's chosen and nothing can compare the greatness of her calling. She is our pride. She is our life our sweetness, our hope, our help and when she in our side nothing but good happens to those who called and pleaded to her.

Despite not receiving nor called to a lofty mission remind yourself that we too are called to respond to our greatest calling and that is to become holy and perfect. Remember, the crown of God awaits those who loves and serve Him and to ignore our greatest calling will also be our greatest loss.

PRAYER:

O holy Mother of the Word Incarnate chosen to be co redeemer of our salvation pray for us sinners and let the fullness of God's graces fall upon the godless, heretics and blasphemers for their conversion that they too will become a part of the Body of Christ your Son so by His death and resurrection will save them from eternal death and be made worthy of the promises of Christ. Amen.

CHAPTER FIVE

UNITY WITH THE FATHER

He, the Almighty had done great things for me and holy is His Name. Actually, Mary's praises to God fell short from the reality of the greatness of His love for her. There is no words to describe the actuality and reality of God's favor to this little insignificant innocent child of Joaquin and Ann chosen to be the mother of our salvation. God groomed Mary as our model. One who imitates her way of life wins God's favor and will received His abundance. We should always give thanks and praise to God for her as our own and great intercessor.

Before the appearance of Gabriel, the archangel, as a little child Mary was taken up and brought up to the presence of the Eternal Father and saw the vision of God's glory and majesty. It was the sight of the Beatific Vision that she instinctively fell prostrate before God's presence. He was surrounded with the splendor of the angelic host that their brilliance was an overwhelming sight unseen anywhere. She revealed to the community what awaits to those who gives all its love to the One who is Love. Paul testified the overwhelming experience himself when he was also taken up to the seventh heaven. He was completely overwhelmed that Paul had no idea wither it was his body or spirit but it was an experience beyond the reality of our mundane existence. But Paul's experience paled beyond what Mary had. Just the vision of God's heavenly host created such majestic aura indescribable. It was a festival of lights revealing the august and perfect beauty of God, her Father. It was written that no one will see the face of God for no one can stand His holiness. A gentle touch from an angel made Mary stood before God's presence and on that moment she was in ecstasy where she could no longer feel or know who she was for His powerful overwhelming presence had separated her soul and spirit from her body. As she was led towards His august majesty, God's kind, adorable and gentle Face and loving eyes became so overwhelmingly captivating and she simply bowed her head, lowered her eyes as she knelt with the greatest reverence before God, her Father. Mary had no more feelings transported to another dimension to an incredible state as if she was absorbed by another being that her union can not be express nor shared. Then she remembered that warmth touch on her head restoring her senses and heard His voice.

"Before I created the world I had chosen you from all my creation, the only one to be greatly exalted and to be honored for all generation to come in the fullness of time and for eternity. Before I formed you in your mother's womb I have chosen you to be the model of creation. I have ordained that you will be my only begotten daughter and specially called to participate in fulfilling my most holy will for all my people. I called you Mary and I have blest you now and for all of time and eternity and I will give to you all my graces and all my favor rest in you now and forever."

God's gentle and loving voice stopped and there followed such serene silence she never experienced before and suddenly there was that beautiful sound of various musical instrument that can not be described but its magical melody was incredibly sweet and gentle. Then, the sound of angelic voices singing glory to God in the highest and peace on earth. The angelic choir filled Mary with indescribable joy and happiness that her face was flooded with tears. The singing continued serenading their future queen and the more she heard them the more it became more beautiful and more appealing that Mary wished it will never end.

Suddenly, she was back to the land of her exile being transported by a host of angels into her home where she heard her father and mother talking to each other. They never knew what their daughter had been. But to Mary it was a shocking change of scenery that she plunged into the deepest darkness. She revealed to the community that it was one of her greatest suffering being separated from her Father in heaven. She wished she could stayed there forever but she had to do His will. Mary was the only privilege creature who saw God face to face and did not die. The experience was unreal and she could not believe she was in heaven body and soul and saw her God and Father. She could not forget His warm touch and His gentle kind voice.

"I have chosen you to be my only begotten daughter."

27

She could not forget His words but at that moment she did not particularly put special meaning knowing that we are all God's children. Sons and daughters of the Most High. But what amazed her was being transported to where the unreachable God was. How could anyone forget seeing God in the fullness of His beauty, glory and majesty. How could she forget the splendor of His throne or His adorable Face. God's kind eyes was so overwhelming and His touch was something Mary will never forget. Seeing the Beatific Vision enlarges the capacity of her little heart and from that moment she was filled with the fire of His love. Once she saw God in the fullness of His glory Mary could never love anything else. Once Mary saw His perfect beauty she could desire anything but God alone. He was her everything. Mary's heart was burning for love of Him. Once she experienced God she could never let go of the fullness of His love. The love she received from Him could not be describe in words or feelings but all she can do was to marvel and enjoy remembering that ecstatic moment Mary was with God. Such love she received from God her Father could never be found in the world, in the universe nor any other creature can give. Even if all creation gathered all its love for her still paled to His love. God's love is the complete possession of something more glorious and more than anything imaginable. How could she forget His perfect beauty God's countenance was so bright beyond description so luminous that the surrounding became a spectacle of unending glorious scenery not found anywhere. How do I deserve such love and favor when I am the lowest among the worms? Mary's humility was the truth that exalted her for all generation and for all eternity.

God, the Almighty who dwells in the highest heaven is not only calling me to participate in His greatest work - transforming creation into His likeness. Our Lady shared to the community that we too are so privilege to have the opportunity to become like God.

"And God said, let us man in our image, after our likeness; and let them have dominion over the fish of the sea, and over the fowl of the air, and over the cattle and over all the earth, and over the fish of the sea, and over the fowl of the air, and over the cattle and over all the earth, and over every creeping thing that creepeth upon the earth." (Genesis 2:26).

Mary felt the drastic changed coming back to the land of our exile. To be in heaven and to be with God was so devastatingly different and she was filled with sadness not knowing when she can see her Father again. Deprived of God's grace and favor the image of God had become a disfigured creature unable to restore itself. Mary's heart was broken seeing God's children struggling to rise beyond their lowliness unable to experience what she had. But Mary knew there is hope that we too can get to heaven and see our God once the Messiah comes. Jesus, her Son will show the way, the truth and the life bringing them consolation and courage to go on and take the narrow way to their heavenly homeland. For now, humanity will have to endure and liked the exiled children of Israel who kept on the journey in order to possessed their promised land. But we are more blest more privileged than the children of Israel for our destination is far greater, far more glorious and far more rewarding since it is the new heaven prepared by God which is more beautiful and more desirable than the old.

Mary, as a devout member of the Jewish religious community joined her parents celebrating the feast of the Passover but her thoughts were preoccupied with her experiences with heaven and her Father. She kept thinking when will she be back to her greatest desire and love, her God the Father in heaven now so distant so unreachable that made her even more sorrowful. Oh how she missed the Beatific Vision and Mary keep trying to recapture that marvelous moment but only intensified her pains and sorrow that she can felt her heart bursting. If you see what Mary saw, you too will understand her brokenness. In Mary's sorrowful moment an angel ministered to her while celebrating Passover that only the Blood of the Most High will save God's people from eternal death. The Blood of the Son of God is an eternal eliminator of all sins past, present and future making mankind eligible to enter the new heaven and will be able to see what Mary saw - the Beatific Vision of God. Thus our Lady of Unity shared what is heaven and what is like to be united with God that even in those brief moments Mary felt it was eternity. But to truly spent eternity with God no words can adequately or properly described it.

Our Lady kept everything in her heart and her presentation to the heavenly Father was the greatest moment in Mary's young life. Unlike the Jewish custom of presenting the first born to the temple, our Lady in her childhood was carried to the place where no other living creature had been so she can be presented to God the Father. Death awaits those who saw the Face of God but only Mary a lowly creature like us saw God face to face transforming her into His likeness. She became God's only begotten daughter chosen to become the greatest participant in our salvation.

Beloved by her Father, God welcome His greatest masterpiece molded from dust and ordained Mary to be blessed among all women and blessed among all creation. She was not to be presented at the temple made by human hands but at the throne of God so she will received the holy anointment and ordination as the most important part in accomplishing God's greatest masterpiece.

If one can truly fathom the fullness of God's grace you will understand what Mary received was beyond the extraordinary. A single grace from God will do great marvelous things to the one who received it but the fullness of God's grace can not be defined. Even the Blessed Virgin Mary failed defining the fullness of God's grace. She could only say, "My soul proclaims the greatness of the Lord. My spirit rejoices in God my savior. For He has looked with favor on His lowly servant. From this day all generations will call me blessed. The Almighty has done great things for me. And holy is His Name."

Mary's magnificat surely failed to described the reality of what is to have the fullness of God's grace. But the truth is, Mary became one with God possessing all that is of God. Chosen to fully participate in the economy of our salvation Mary understood why the cross is the only way that all of us can possess God and heaven. Mary was the first to follow God's command to pick up the cross and carry it. There will never be any other creature who suffered so much sadness and sorrows than Mary once she was brought back to the land of our exile. The valley of tears. Even worst, Mary's knowledge that she will bear the Messiah and the revelation that the Blood of her only Son will be shed for mankind's redemption brought more sufferings than anyone could bear. To shed one's blood is certain death and Mary suffered severe anxiety of the coming of Jesus' Passion and crucifixion. Let the world know that God's beloved daughter suffered intensely and continuously much like God's own begotten Son.

The Catholic Church alone honored and revered the Blessed Virgin Mary for her never ending works for our salvation. And it would be one's greatest benefits and advantage to have both God's Son and daughter to be on our side to ensure our salvation. Two powerful intercessors is definitely and absolutely better than one.

REFLECTION:

"And the Word was made flesh, and dwelt among us, (And we beheld his glory, the glory as of the only begotten of the Father) Full of grace and truth." (1 John 1:14).

As Jesus was the only begotten Son of the Father, Mary though a creature born of Joaquin and Ann was raised to the highest honor any creature will ever receive when God's ordaining action claimed her as His only begotten daughter. Although made of corruptible and susceptible flesh the Triune God had no other alternative but to ordained Mary as His only begotten daughter to made possible the greatness of God's project in transforming dust into divinity. The Triune God is in great need of one solitary soul, a creature who can help Him transforming dust to divinity. Human logic can never fathom this greatest mystery, our creation and our relationship with the Creator. Who will He chose. It was easy for God for He fully knew Mary and by the Triune God's dispensation she then received the fullness of God. Although Mary had been greatly honored and revered by the Catholic faithful, billions does not. Even their Christian brothers who bolted from the true church marginalized her greatness by simply invalidating Mary's fiat. Billions had no clue that by honoring and glorifying a mere creature like Mary the Holy Trinity will also be greatly honored and glorified.

The human race should put her on the highest pedestal because she was chosen by the Almighty God for our sake. It was the incorruptible flesh of Mary that received God's life forming a new creation design to make possible in fulfilling His plan. Finally, the Word was made flesh and it has to be the sinless flesh of His only begotten daughter Mary that His Son of the Most High will be conceived. Royalty begot royalty thus the Holy Spirit can only be wedded to the royal lineage Mary received from the Father's gifting of the fullness of His grace. And the divine life of God was incorporated into His chosen daughter transforming Mary into a divine offspring though made of flesh. One of the marvelous privilege when one received the fullness of God.

Since the Son of God was from heaven He cannot possibly be conceive in the land of our exile but only on a womb prepared and groomed in heaven. As Mary was presented to the Father in heaven while a child, her return to earth was to fulfill His Father's will. As her Son Jesus said, No one can come to the Father except through me and the same divine principle can be applied to Mary that no one can come to the Triune God except through her and the Son.

PRAYER:

Immaculate daughter of the Most High God behold us, children of Eve suffering from the curses of sin, intercede for us to your beloved Father in heaven that we too, His afflicted exiled children maybe healed from this deadly disease that keeps spreading to the whole human race. As our mother and model, pray for us for the graces of our true conversion so we too can be transform into your likeness and also to the likeness of the Triune God giving Him the greatest honor and glory through you. Amen.

CHAPTER SIX
. . . .
WITH HER SON

Progress eased everything in the land of our exile. Our life now is more bearable and even comfortable compared what they suffered in the past. Initially, our first parents and the succeeding generations suffered much after their eviction from Eden but God gave us a brain able to create, imagine, analyze and think to the highest imaginable. God gave us soul having the mind, intellect and understanding providing us the greatest tool for survival in a very difficult and challenging environment. Even though God was angry with our first parent's disobedience He did not took away our brain equip with so much power potential. Such was and is the goodness of our great God.

In the garden of Eden God abundantly gave Adam and Eve everything they needed. Fruits of all kinds, delicious vegetation and variety of meat, poultry and fishes in the ocean for food. All Adam had to do was to take care of what God had given Him. Simply, a steward of His garden.

"And the Lord God took the man, and put him into the garden of Eden to dress it and keep it." (Genesis 2:15).

Such was and is the generosity of God. Knowing of Adam's need that he was lonely, God gave him a companion and helper to make him happier. God knows our needs and He never failed in taking great care of us even if we think the contrary. Despite of all God had done for them, they disobeyed Him resulting in our exile. Punished, we inherited all kinds of sufferings, pains, sorrows, afflictions, physical and mental infirmities and worse, our mortality. But God's goodness remained as our brain power were able to invent and improvise to make life easier and manageable. In the stone age, the human brain invented the wheel. Then as time passed by we developed our brain into a powerful mechanism that rapidly changed our environment developing modern technology in all field of endeavor making our exile more tolerable and even desirable. In our progressive society, many acquired great wealth and riches that they can easily acquired an isolated island and making it their own paradise. We were evicted in the garden of Eden but the brain God gave had produced a magical world thus making our exile less painful. In fact, we are so used living in our world that modern medicine are spending time, talent and resources trying to extend lives longer. Such desire to live longer or even eternally here on earth validates that we are now enjoying what is in our world. Most of us even chose the world that society exerted the greatest effort to make the world even better. Perhaps, we are trying to recapture what was lost in the garden of Eden. In the modern world, we may even think that we have a much better place than Eden.

But for God's chosen daughter, her exile was very painful that the separation from the Eternal Father became a torment worse than hell itself. Being with God and seeing all of Him was the greatest inexpressible joy and happiness she even had experience. The world to her became a desolated undesirable place even repulsive in her sight. Although Mary belongs to the tribe of God's chosen people she saw their afflictions and infirmities deforming the beautiful image of their God. The comparison between heaven and earth has none. Our Lady's memory of God surrounded by the heavenly host remained fresh. The angels were so perfectly created that their beauty and countenance can easily be mistaken as that of the Most High. They were clothed with the brilliance of the sun so pleasing and appealing to behold. The vision of God and heaven was so overwhelming that she had no desire at all to come back.

The sound she heard was the most beautiful music with the angelic choir accompanied by many musical instruments she never heard before wishing it never ends. Once she heard the sound of music here on earth, our Lady experienced irritating noise of disorganized tune of defective voice and instrument which added to her sufferings. Mary's exile was worse than the exile of Adam and Eve.

The sight of dry desert land made her more sad for it was so difficult to forget the face to face encounter with God. All earthly beauty and splendor turn to ugliness compared to what she saw in God and heaven. Earth is truly the land of our exile. The angels which our Lady saw were so brilliantly beautiful but once she saw His Face they lose their brilliance. She could not describe the beauty and splendor of God. Although she alone saw God face to face during her presentation, our Lady could not described to her community simply for the reason that it is impossible.

There is no suffering greater than our Lady suffered after her presentation to God and she tried to find ways much like us to ease the pain. She went to her little garden considered pleasant with so many flowers blossoming giving her a small piece of consolation. She picked a rose and smelt its sweet aroma but sadness filled her heart again as she remembered those heavenly scent that captivated her while she was prostrate before the throne of her Father. She had never smelt such aroma a smell that was heavenly perfume. What an unpleasant place our Lady's exile in the land of the living. What an offensive odor we all have to smell in this world filled with filth and refused. What a mighty difference was the odor of heaven where its fragrance filled her soul with sweetness. She revealed to the community that in heaven one will become a part of it transforming the soul into a perfect, glorious and beautiful being making itself a part of God enjoying what is perfect happiness and inexpressible joy that never ends. What Paul described in his writing about the seventh heaven is so far from its reality since to be integrated with God simply cannot be put into words but by experience only.

From day one after Mary's presentation, our Lady's heart was pierced by the sword which penetrated her innermost being. Mary's soul was pierced with much sorrow and sadness being separated from her Father in heaven not knowing when she will be with Him. She confided to the community that there is no sorrow and pain that can compare to what she had to endure. The separation from her beloved Father was worse than death and even hell. But she did not mind to undergo such severe suffering again if only she can be back to where she was. But she cannot and Mary had no choice but to do His will. She knew God intimately for Mary kept in her heart, be still and know that I am God. She embraced and endured her cross until the archangel Gabriel appeared to her that she will bear the Messiah in her virginal womb.

"The Holy Spirit shall come upon thee, and the power of the Highest shall overshadow thee; therefore also that holy thing which shall be born of thee be called the Son of God." (Luke 1:35).

The annunciation became a feast for the church to immortalized the extraordinary event as the beginning period of our redemption, sanctification and salvation. Finally at last, the long awaited coming of a savior prophesied is near at hand. Our Lady's new mission did alleviate her pains and sorrows knowing that God's own Son, the God who chose her as its own daughter will dwell in her womb. Joy consumed Mary realizing that God unites Himself to her, a worthless creature.

"Then said Mary unto the angel, how shall this be seeing I know not man?" (Luke 1:34).

She initially challenged the messenger but possessing the fullness of God's grace she was quick in discerning that it was God's will and choice and as an obedient daughter, Mary quickly responded and her yes was heard like the loudest thunder and heaven and earth rejoices knowing that the Almighty God was so pleased with her. Of course, it is God's perfect choice that Mary will be the perfect partner in reclaiming His lost children.

Once the Holy Spirit entered into her womb, with the conception of the Messiah completely change the condition of our Lady. She was greatly relieved of her suffering and found the greatest joy of being with God and heaven. The experience was not the same but it was her greatest joy and happiness to bear God's only begotten Son in her womb. Slowly, the experienced she had during her presentation came back to here. She felt that heaven and God came down from His glorious throne so the Triune God will dwell in her. Now, she could not find the words to describe what it is like to be completely possessed God.

She instructed the community that if any one could experience what she had, one will never commit a sin. She taught that even though we are mere creature capable of only offending God we should never get discourage in striving to always do God's will. By doing so, she added, one will experience the inexpressible joy of having God presence in the soul. Our Lady emphasized that all the pains and sufferings will always be with us for it was His ordaining will but we should never allow ourselves to be consumed to those moments but rather looked beyond this life. She reminded how much Bernadette of Lourdes did suffered from all kinds of trials and afflictions sending her close to despair but I assured her that we all have to endure and embrace whatever happen for this is our greatest and highest good. To accept and embrace His will. By doing so, we have given God the greatest pleasure when we participate carrying the cross for it is the only way we can be intimately united to the Triune God.

"I cannot promise you happiness in this life but on the next."

She reminded us how her devoted child was greatly consoled and Bernadette did learned how to embraced whatever trials and tribulations she encountered by focusing her sight on eternity. We were also reminded how we too can also by detaching ourselves from earthly desires and focus faithfully on her promise to live our lives based on the teachings of her Son and she will help us gain the crown that she now wears. In this life's journey nothing is easy. There is not a day that we are free from some kind of burden that weighed our soul. She reminded us their great burden by suddenly fleeing the comfort of their home in order to go to Egypt once the angel warned them of the danger of losing her Son by staying since an order was executed by King Herod that every newborn child must die.

Our Lady had another burden how to break the news to a holy man like Joseph that she was carrying a child which was not his. It was also a very hard and trying time for a just and righteous man like Joseph to turn Mary over knowing the strict religious community will stone her to death for having an illegitimate child. They both suffered greatly for answering God's call but it is also a great reminder to us that God is always there to help and protect His chosen ones. For example, an angel comforted Joseph not to fear marrying Mary.

Mary was completely at peace knowing she was doing God's will and to be stone to death by carrying an illegitimate child she considered a great grace - to die for her God. But she also knew it will never happened because God's perfect plan cannot be accomplished if she and her Child dies.

But what was amazing was her teaching that for every great pains and sufferings if received with love follows great consolation and joy. Most important, one receives more graces. She then told us when they were traveling during the harsh and cold wintry day tired and wearied they could not find a place to stay. She felt the weariness and fatigued for carrying her Child ready to be delivered. They were anxious but again God fully with them they were able to find rest on the stable sufficient enough to have their rest. Such providence will always be available to His chosen ones.

There on Bethlehem where the greatest miracle occurred - the virgin birth. Contrary to our own natural birth, the Messiah's entrance to our world was totally supernatural. The Infant Child leaped out of her womb scaring not our Lady's virginal flesh and she saw the stable turning into a place much like she saw when our Lady was presented. She shared with us how the stable was transformed into a palatial place. Mary saw heaven's glory, again seeing her heavenly Father appearing with a multitude of angelic host but this time our Lady could not see God's Face for its brilliance fully covered His holy and majestic Presence. It was like a festival unseen unheard unbelievable!!! It was for a moment - heaven on earth. Our Lady heard the beautiful voices of God's heavenly host.

"And suddenly there was with the angel a multitude of the heavenly host praising God and saying. Glory to God in the highest, and on earth peace, good will toward." (Luke 2:13).

She saw the radiant beauty of her Son illuminated with heavenly lights and Mary's joy transported her into another dimension that once again she felt her oneness with God the Father and oneness with the Messiah. She could no longer feel her own body for her soul and spirit soared towards the unreachable God. She could not find the words to describe what she had experience being united with God. She related that to be in heaven is not the ultimate joy and happiness but it is only through the oneness and our own assimilation with the Almighty God. Anyone who had such experience will lose all its desire to live in the world. Our Lady confided she wanted to remain to that state of ecstasy for all of eternity.

"This is my beloved Son born of a woman to whom I am most pleased."

She heard the most pleasing voice uttered by her Father.

And suddenly everything change and he saw the stable in its original state and Mary felt the cold and dampness of the tiny place. With the swaddling clothes, Mary wrapped her Son and gently laid Him on the manger. But her joy remained and its intensity slowly diminished much like the natural joy of a loving and caring mother to its first and only child.

"And there were in the same country shepherds abiding in the field, keeping watch over their flock by night. And lo, the angel of the Lord came upon them and the glory of the Lord shone around them; and they were sore afraid." (Luke 2:8-9).

The shepherds fear turned into joy as they went to Bethlehem excited to see the long awaited savior Christ, the Lord.

"And they came with haste, and found Mary, ands Joseph and the babe lying in a manger." (Luke 2:16).

They were filled with joy once they saw their new born king clothed not in royal attire but in swaddling clothes. They were amazed when they saw the light of heaven shining on the holy Infant. The shepherds saw that this Child does not need the greatest palace as its birth place for they were enlightened that this is their God who is above all gods and they rejoiced to be in His Presence.

"And they they had seen it, they made known abroad the saying which was told them concerning this child." (Luke 2:17).

Our Lady blest them knowing the most lowly in society were called and chosen to tell the world that Christ had come reminding us that God has the tendency in choosing the most lowly. Like Mary, she too was the most lowly handmaid chosen among all women to become God's partner in the salvation of His creation. She was chosen to be mother of God and what she had experienced with the Triune God she kept all in her heart.

"But Mary keep all these things, and pondered them in her heart." (Luke 2:19).

REFLECTION:

"For unto you is born this day in the city of David a savior, which is Christ the Lord." (Luke 2:11).

Chosen by the Father to be the mother of His Son Mary was always united with her Son. In the mind of God was conceived that He will come into the land of our exile through the holiest of place and that can only be done in the holy womb of His daughter. He as the Second Persona must clothed Himself with human flesh so God can reveal Himself to the world that He has come to make peace. But God cannot simply took on a flesh that is corruptible and enslave with sin. The flesh that God must put on must be absolutely holy, perfect, pure, spotless, undefiled and immaculate and only Mary His daughter can provide. Jesus, the Son of Mary and the Son of God cannot be separated in its essence. Jesus is both God and man. He is God because He came down from heaven but had to be conceived in the flesh of man through Mary and such combining genetic elements delivered the offsprings of the new covenant. God and man had become one through this holy merger designed by the Father. As Jesus will be our Savior, Mary who was and is always united with her Son cannot be deleted from the eternal union making her truly co redeemer with Jesus, her one and only begotten Son through God's Third Persona.

PRAYER

Holy Mary mother of God who conceived the long awaited Messiah pray for us that your Son's redeeming work be not in vain by obtaining from His Sacred Heart the fullness of His mercy for our grievous sin of negligence and ingratitude by our failure in living His life on us. Look with pity on us sinful children of Eve and help us in obtaining from your divine Son all the graces necessary for our conversion so that we maybe made worthy of His love and gain eternal happiness and joy in heaven. Amen.

Our Lady of Unity Chosen by the Father to bear His Son and chosen by the Holy Spirit to be His spouse, pray for us sinners that we too maybe united with the Triune God now and forever. Amen.

CHAPTER SEVEN
. . . .
WITH HER SPOUSE

Our Lady shared to the community that her own betrothal was part of God's calling in fulfilling His will. Although she preferred to remain a virgin our Lady never contradicted what was God's plan for her while on earth. Joaquin and Ann were the perfect couple chosen by God to be the parents and guardian of God's beloved daughter. The example of her holy parents that marriage can bring happiness by how they loved and cared for each other offered some consoling thoughts but having experienced God and heaven during her presentation our Lady simply could not love any other creature nor any man. She knew her whole being belongs to God alone and to have any weighs heavily on Mary's heart and soul. Our Lady knew that in marriage husband and wife must become one. Like her mother, Ann, she must give all to her husband knowing that God's will be done. Mary must make room for her husband though painful she must embraced God's plan. Again, our Lady must bear the burden of her cross. She felt anxiety that she could not attain the standard of her mother Anne as a wife to Joseph.

Mary knew that her very own mother's sanctity was so great because of the many graces that God bestowed upon her. Anne's very name signifies "grace". God prepared her with many gifts and graces. It should be expected since God's work and selection are perfect and it was natural to expect that God should make Anne a worthy mother of the purest creature who will represent humanity's own deficiency.

Anne was zealous in performing good works and always striving for virtue. She loved God sincerely, and always resigned to His holy will. Mary's parents suffered for Anne sterility was for twenty years. Our

Lady saw how faithful Anne was in fulfilling perfectly her vocation as a mother and wife. She too was blessed among women for Anne was the grandmother of our Lord and God the Father favored her so much also because Anne bore in her womb God's most favored daughter Mary. Anne served God perfectly for she was a perfect mother and trained Mary to the path of sanctity.

Since Mary kept everything in her heart she was bothered remembering of her betrothal to the Third Persona of God, the Holy Spirit. As a young innocent child and favored by the Most High she understood that in God along she will be wed. Her appearance before the Father in heaven during the presentation was also Mary's betrothal to the Holy Spirit. As a young girl before her Father's throne in heaven Our Lady was confirmed and divinely ordained to be God's only begotten daughter and to be betrothed spouse of the Holy Spirit.

Mary's betrothal to Joseph became another heavy cross on her.

"To a virgin espoused to a man whose name was Joseph of the house of David: and the virgin's name was Mary." (Luke 1:27).

To be betrothed twice was a constant terrifying temptation in Mary's pure mind. If God is such a jealous God then why is it that I will be given to a man as a wife. She tried to make sense of her depressing dilemma. Worse it is against God's commandment to be married to two husbands. Silently in her pure soul the troubling dilemma kept tormenting Mary but it did not take long receiving enlightenment from her heavenly Spouse that her double betrothal was of two purpose. One was divine and the other was human designed by God to accomplish His plan in merging God and man.

Our Lady understood that her betrothal to the Third Persona of God was heavenly where her whole being physical and spiritual became one with God. This is the kind of marriage signifying the perfect union of God and His creation. It was God's design that to accomplish the union of God and His creation there is great and essential need to recreate the works of His Hands and this can only be by first the complete and permanent indwelling of the Holy Spirit on a creature so by this union of two elements of diverse nature will harmonized into one. Thus, the union of Mary and the Holy Spirit conceived something so special beyond earthly but only made possible by God's design. The birth of God formed in Mary's womb came into existence a new creation of God and man as one. Christ Jesus was God from the genetic makeup of God the Holy Spirit and He is also man from the genetic makeup of Mary.

Our Lady's community were taught that the indwelling of the Holy Spirit is God's great gift to His people and anyone can become His dwelling place. But such soul must live a blameless and holy life pleasing to God. However, such gift of the indwelling of the Holy Spirit cannot be sustain for the stain of sin or the curses of sin have irrevocably infected our being thus His indwelling is merely temporal. But the indwelling of the Holy Spirit in our Lady's soul was not temporal but perpetual since our Lady was espoused to Him forever.

Since Mary was conceived without sin, Our Lady will never be subjected to slavery of sin. The Holy Spirit will never leave anyone who does not commit sin and it was divinely fitting that His spouse was totally free from it. Meanwhile, we could never have complete or permanent possession of the Holy Spirit because we are powerless in conquering that enslaves us. A great example was God's own favorite and chosen servant David whose very own heart was like of God but fell miserably from our slavery to sin. By committing the sin of sloth, lust and adultery David became repulsive in God's eyes and the Holy Spirit departed from his soul. David's own son had the privilege of conversing to God also failed miserably by worshipping and embracing other worthless god. We knew Solomon was the wisest of all men for God granted him the gift of wisdom which came from the Holy Spirit but sin overcame him and the Holy Spirit departed from him. The same thing with Moses the great prophet of Israel who spoke to God all the time but was not able to reached the promised land because he failed God. In the modern times we saw how priests, ministers, pastors, preachers and servants of God first filled with the Holy Spirit became victims to our sinful nature. Therefore, we should never boast that we are filled with the Holy Spirit for it is not a guarantee that He will remain with the soul. It is the inconstancy of our being that the Holy Spirit easily comes and goes. It takes the fullness of God's graces which meant full of God that His Spirit remains forever. Our Lady having the fullness of His grace was filled with God because it was so necessary and essential that Mary and God become one not only in time but also in eternity. And since our Lady was merely a creature like us she needed all of God's graces for without it she could not permanently and perpetually united with the Triune God. She must remain pure, spotless, immaculate, perfect and holy otherwise the Holy Spirit will depart from her risking the work of God. Mary is not subject for punishment since she was sinless and our Lady need not to be redeemed like us for she had been anointed and specially chosen to be the Eternal Father's only daughter free from original sin. Indeed, Mary was conceived without sin is our greatest pride and honor.

Before being betrothed to Joseph, Mary was betrothed to the Third Persona of God, the Holy Spirit. The Eternal Father in His infinite wisdom groomed His daughter in the fullness of her humanity to be espoused to His Third Persona in the fullness of His divinity so the consummation of the union will produced the perfect model for humanity so it can be transformed into the likeness of the model of God's renovated creation. Therefore, the double betrothal of Mary was divinely designed for the perfection of His purpose. Both Mary and Joseph did suffered when the holy man Joseph found out that Mary was pregnant.

"Now the birth of Jesus Christ was on this wise; when as his mother Mary was espoused to Joseph before they came together she was found with child of the Holy Ghost." (Matthew 1:1).

Put any man in Joseph's shoes and the reaction would surely be extremely distressing. Most would probably in rage knowing that his bride to be was carrying somebody's child. Every man would react differently but most men would judge such woman ill refute. In the Jewish religious community had Joseph exposed our Lady she would have been stone to death.

"Then Joseph her husband, being a just man, and not willing to make publick example was minded to put her away privily." (Matthew 1:19).

Such goodness and kindness exhibited by Joseph should not surprise us because he was chosen by God to be Mary's husband here on earth. God knew what Joseph was made of. To be the head and protector of the holy family God chose the best in Joseph. He was Mary's greatest supporter and protector, a witness to her perpetual virginity having never soiled nor defiled the precious jewel of his God. Chosen like Mary but lesser known in our salvation history, Joseph's sanctity was great to be worthy of such calling. Joseph's marital union with Mary was divine, a union of heart, soul and spirit preserving the purity of their being abstaining from physical union as to serve and to protect God's holy will. The Most High holy God will never permit any shadow of sin to contaminate His immaculate daughter, His chosen mother and His chosen spouse, to do so compromises the holiness of God. To think of Joseph and Mary entering into physical union is ungodly and even beastly for the womb of Mary was more than holy. If Moses was commanded to take off his sandal before the ground where God was present then no one should ever marginalized Mary to be defiled by any man. Mary's womb was more than hallowed ground. It was the birthplace of God.

Therefore Joseph was chosen to be the stand in for her one true spouse of the Holy Spirit. Joseph was chosen to protect her and his step Son from all kinds of evil. Even before Joseph knew that Mary was carrying God's Son he was given the grace to be our Lady's protector by not exposing her to the religious community. And it was Joseph who protected the life of the Messiah by his diligent and concern for the holy family.

"And when they were departed, behold the angel of the Lord appeared to Joseph in a dream, saying, Arise, and take the young child and his mother, and flee into Egypt, and be thou there until I bring thee word; for Herod will seek the young child to destroy him."

Most of us cannot see the greatness of this man, Joseph, who was chosen among all men to be the guardian, guide and protector of our Lord and Savior Jesus Christ and to our Lady. Joseph did no great preaching and teaching but his servitude to God was unequal. Sacred Scriptures revealed the greatness of God's other prominent prophets. They preached God's Word eloquently drawing many to hear them and they were exalted as great servants of God but in the final analysis what Joseph did deserves the highest honor for his silent role in our redemption and salvation. St. Joseph never said a single word like those great prophets and preachers who wowed and seduced its audience with their charisma. But Joseph was way above them all. Like a lamb lead to the slaughter, he answered his calling in silence, solitude, strength and sacredness. He said no word but did everything perfectly in action. This is the kind of servant God so admired and Joseph was far exalted in the highest heaven and he received the greatest reward with his impressive performance before the eyes of his Maker. He was perfect in doing God's will.

As step father of Jesus, he did everything he could to be the perfect father. Joseph provided our Lord shelter and he labored as a lowly carpenter earning honestly so he can provide for his family. Day in and day out until his last breath St. Joseph fulfilled his greatest vocation as the provider and head of God's beloved and he never failed his family. And Joseph never failed his God. Tracing his heritage, St. Joseph came from distinguished royalty. He was an offspring of King David and King Solomon two of the greatest ruler of Israel. Although both were chosen by God they both failed Him miserably and it is also our great reminder never to take God's grace for granted and to always remember His holy commandments and to live always in His Presence. In God's eyes, Joseph towered over his more famous and exalted royal lines of David and Solomon. They made the tribe of Israel great and famous. They conquered all their enemies. Solomon built the greatest temple ever constructed by human hands and both kings were revered and exalted. Certainly, they were good and faithful servants of God for the great things they accomplished for God.

But the lesser known Joseph who lived not in palaces but in a tiny house who worked hard as a lowly carpenter for their sustenance providing the hidden God all His needs. St Joseph did not built the greatest temple of God like Solomon but with his strong hands he raised the Savior of mankind and the mother of God. The world may not recognized the greatness of this lowly carpenter but he was in the eyes of God.

As head of the holy family, St. Joseph established the type of one holy church before it was ordained and commissioned by his step Son. He truly was the greatest patriarch and St. Joseph deserves our greatest respect and recognition as the greatest saint of God next to his beloved wife, Mary, the greatest lady of our race.

Although the Holy Spirit was the only one true Spouse of Mary, Joseph did received the gifts of wisdom, understanding, knowledge, counsel, fortitude, piety and the fear of the Lord making him the perfect holy husband for God's beloved daughter never defiling the dwelling place of the Messiah. As Mary was always united to the Holy Spirit, Joseph likewise is also united to Him for without this union may derail the plan of our redemption. It was God's will that Mary's womb and persona should never be defiled nor corrupted in time and eternity for if it is so then she will failed God and like Eve she will follow her destruction.

"If any man defile the temple of God, him shall God destroy; for the temple of God is holy, which temple ye are." (Corinthians 3:17).

Thus Joseph united with the Holy Spirit did his job in protecting and preserving Mary's virginity and immaculacy for she was God's greatest temple.

REFLECTION

"Know ye not that ye are the temple of God, and that the Spirit of God dwelleth in you?" (I Corinthians 3:16).

Our greatest challenges is to truly believe that our bodies belongs to God and such conviction had become our greatest obstacle to live a holy and perfect life. In the world we live in adulteries, fornication and sexual perversions had become a thrilling and exciting passion thus we have indeed desecrated what belongs to God. God willed that we should multiply ourselves like the multitude of stars in the skies because He will be greatly glorified and honored if all of us become like Him. Thus, the sacrament of matrimony was instituted so God's offsprings multiplies providing a multitude of divine seedlings ready to sprout into His likeness once God's grace is applied in their lives.

But the physical union between man and woman in marriage have been marginalized into a self gratifying experience not knowing that God's intention was the production of offsprings for His benefits. The pleasure of sex became a dominating dilemma that constantly enflame the passion of our flesh to seek as much satisfaction it can get while defeating the life of the spirit. When this happens, we desecrated God's temple and if we persist in our lustful passion then there is no way the Holy Spirit will dwell in the sinful soul. Paul, the greatest apostle preached constantly and repeatedly that our bodies is God's Body and we have to become the best baby sitter ever so to speak to ensure that God's body will not be destroyed through our recklessness and negligences in taking care of God's own life in us. We have to constantly remind ourselves that the Holy Spirit desires to dwell in us but we must make our bodies pure, chaste and undefiled so He can come in and live with us.

PRAYER:

Our Lady of Unity chosen by the Father to be the mother of God pray for us that your Divine Spouse will enkindle our hearts to love what is truth accepting the teachings of Holy mother church that the sacrament of holy matrimony will be held in utmost reverence that husbands and wives will love each other as Christ loves the Church, His Body. Amen.

CHAPTER EIGHT
. . . .
WITH HER CHURCH

"And I saw the new heaven and a new earth; for the first heaven and the first earth were passed away; and there was no more sea." (Revelation 21:1).

We were enlightened by our Lady that the first earth were the most difficult of times and those who dwelt on it suffered greatly simply of their deprivation of knowing her Son. Although they knew God existed His revelation of Himself was not in full. This is one of the greatest reason why His chosen ones like Moses, David, Solomon and others failed their God even though they frequently conversed with Him. Our first parents were also in constant contact with Him and also failed miserably.

They failed God because they were deprived of the Word made flesh. No one showed them the way, the truth and the life. The fullness of God's truth was revealed to the whole world but the world did not knew Him. They have their own lives and the world become an attraction enslaving creation to seek the greatest satisfaction possible. In the world, the life of the spirit is repulsive while living fully in the flesh brings the greatest pleasure. Like in Sodom and Gomorrah, they strive solely to experience the greatest pleasure for their flesh. When this happens God vaguely exists in their lives. The Holy Spirit have completely disappeared from their soul since the raging passion of the flesh forces Him to flee. Knowing the hardships and difficulties of His creation God have no other choice but to personally get involved in fixing and helping us how we can triumph over the enemies of our salvation. Thus in His infinite wisdom, God's Second Persona must enter into our world so by His Presence He can perfectly teach and show us how to win over sin and death. And to make His Presence perpetual God established the church and by doing it the new earth was brought into fruition replacing the old earth which have detained many of God's children in Limbo waiting for a long time for the expected coming of the Messiah who will opened the promised new heaven.

The absence of Jesus was the main reason why God's chosen people persistently failed Him. Despite receiving the Ten Commandments of God, Moses, David, Solomon and other prominent religious leaders at that time kept on stumbling and failing God's holy will. They did obeyed and observed God's commandments and precepts religiously but through legalism and not by pure and perfect love. It is only through the pure and perfect love taught and shown by Jesus that God's holy will be fulfilled. As mentioned before, The Pharisees religiously observed and followed God's commandments to the letter of the law and even added more to it but still God was not satisfied. The one way He can truly be pleased to the highest and greatest level was only through the example of Jesus pure and perfect love manifested in how He lived His life with us. All God's chosen servants could not attained holiness and perfection for they were greatly deprived of the Teacher of perfect love. The coming of Jesus renewed everything and the new covenant became the saving standard for those who truly want to be holy and perfect like God. The old covenant can never accomplished in transforming God's creation in His likeness. He must introduced something more dramatic and dynamic to accomplished His greatest plan. The coming of Jesus renewed and revived everything and the new covenant became the saving standard for those who truly want to become like Him. The new covenant truly and really brought down the Almighty God and did the most dirtiest work in order to justify, redeem, reconcile and finally our greatest reward the salvation of our wretched soul. And even with the involvement of the Messiah, still His tremendous sacrifice and even His death came up short unless God's other Persona, the Holy Spirit get involved. Therefore, a monotheistic God despite of all His power and might can never complete His greatest masterpiece unless He had His Three Persona working as One. This is how hard and impossible will be our transformation to become like God. He must really and truly worked three times harder in order for us to become like Him. God had to because it is not that simple and easy to make God out of that worthless dust. It was much so easier for God to make the great constellation, the earth, the moon and the entire cosmos because He simply open His mouth.

"Let there be light"

And there was the light and the whole universe easily came into existence.

But transforming dust into divinity was a completely different matter and God the Father alone can not do it. He must have His Son and the Holy Spirit getting heavily involved to accomplished our majestic and magical transformation so to speak. It is logical the existence of the Triune God.

As the new earth begins its reign the first heaven became extinct. It had to be destroyed for Lucifer and his followers desecrated it by their disobedience and rebellion towards God. The old heaven was not at all perfect nor a desirable place because Lucifer had contaminated it with his evil desire to replace God with himself.

"And there was war in heaven; Michael and his angels fought against the dragon; and the dragon fought and his angels. And prevailed not; neither was their place found anymore in heaven." (Revelation 12:7-8).

Once Lucifer and his legions were defeated they were casted away from heaven into the world. Heaven swiftly became hell. Lucifer's eviction from heaven was worse than Adam and Eve. He could no longer enjoy all the beauty, splendor and glory of heaven. But his greatest loss was God. Losing heaven and God is losing everything. Lucifer had lost love, peace, joy, beauty, goodness, kindness and perfection and he was transformed into a raging foaming ugly demon filled with anger, hatred, jealousy and that extreme unexplainable pain and misery that made him a restless wandering wounded beast looking to destroy everything so to ease and relieve his unbearable burden he must eternally endure. Once the most beautiful of God's creation, the former prince of angel became the most horrific sight and he was more enraged seeing his own repulsiveness. Knowing he could no longer possessed heaven, Satan in his raging anger vowed to destroy God's creation. He will never stop working hard that we will also have the same fate joining Satan in his own everlasting kingdom where anger, hatred, cruelty and all kinds of evil will be its company. There is no more hope or any chance to be restored into the company of God and His saints.

Once Lucifer and his followers were expelled from the first heaven they immediately claimed earth as their temporary dwelling place. Like us, they became our temporary companion in the world until the final judgement is exercised. While awaiting for their assignment to hell Satan made the world their own heaven knowing that later on they will be condemned in the worst possible place one could imagine, hell. Our Lady showed the three little children during her apparition at Fatima, a horrible vision of hell which terrified them and innocently offered themselves to her so that souls will not be lost to eternal perdition. Satan embraced his temporary exile in the world by deceiving and destroying as many as he can in order to hurt God and to prevent us from possessing what he coveted the most, heaven. Satan knew how dreadful and miserable hell is and he loves to bring as many as he could to accompany him.

As the cliche goes, misery loves company. It is Satan's greatest mission to prevent God's children from entering heaven thinking that we are not deserving. In his excessive pride and arrogance, Satan still think he' alone deserves to be in heaven and no one else. Thus, Satan and his legions filled with anger and jealousy have been raging with fiery vengeance on us. And our Lady's Son warned us about our dangerous powerful enemies.

"Be sober, be vigilant; because your adversary the devil, is a roaring lion, walketh about, seeking whom he may devour." (1Peter 5:8).

Our Lady kept reminding our community to keep our sight to the most Holy Trinity for each powerful Persona will be our greatest protector and partner in defeating all the enemies of our salvation. She taught us to think constantly of God the Father's Presence that He is always looking at us. We should keep in our hearts that we are specially created for Him and not for anyone else. When we do so, to live a blameless and holy life is much easier to do. As we are united to God the Father always think of His Second Persona, God the Son, Jesus our Lord who came down to give up His life for our sake. As His redeemed, we became a part of His Body with the greatest privilege to receive those powerful sacraments so our union with Christ will never be broken. As we are one with Christ think always of God's Third Persona the Holy Spirit for He is the one who will perfectly finish the works of God. Keep reminding not to grieve the Holy Spirit by committing serious sins so He will not leave from you. Once the Holy Spirit dwells in us so does the Triune God. Such unity makes the soul strongly secure with Him.

Our Lady's instruction if followed will receive God's graces and that our constant unity with the most Holy Trinity will never be broken unless of course one chose to do so by sin. Responder to her calling will be consecrated and dedicated to the Triune God and such unity will be forever unless the responder renounced the holy bonding. Our Lady revealed the blessed benefits of being consecrated to the Triune God.

When one is consecrated to the First Person, God the Father, one will be received by Him immediately became His special children chosen to participate in Our Lady's final mission. Once consecrated to Him, God will never allow the consecrated one to be separated from Him unless one decided to break from the Triune God and from her community. Consecrated souls of our Lady's community have God's full protection like He protected the righteous servant Job.

"And the Lord said unto Satan, Behold, all that he hath is in thy power; only upon himself put not thine hand. So Satan went forth from the presence of the Lord." (Job 1:12).

As Job's story went Satan did everything to destroy Job and his family. In addition, Satan took all his wealth and his health but he remained faithful to God. We may not be tried like Job but it is in faithfulness and steadfastness that one will receive the greatest of his blessings and full protection from all evils.

When one is consecrated to His Second Persona, our Lord Jesus Christ will be its perpetual guide to the way, the truth and the life. Our Lord will walk with the soul so the journey to the narrow path will be much easier and tolerable.

He will always remind you to keep on going never giving up the race. Being consecrated to Him brings the greatest assurance that He will never leave you and will keep feeding and nourishing you with Himself so victory will be achieve over sin, Satan and death.

"I am the living bread which came down from heaven; if any man eat this bread, he shall live forever; and the bread that I will give is my flesh, which I will give for the life of the world." (St. John 6:5).

Our Lady's most powerful instruction was to attend daily Mass. She revealed that heaven lowered itself in order to participate and adoring the completion of the works of the Holy Trinity in union with His Body, the church. Most baptized Catholics could not truly fathom the great mystery of how Holy Mass protects and preserve the world and its people. God is being reminded each time a Holy Mass is celebrated of the pure and perfect love of His Son. Most importantly, the Holy Mass preserves and perpetuates our justification, redemption and our salvation. And the greatest benefit from Holy Mass is the reception of the real Body and

Blood of our Lord Jesus cementing the unity of the baptized Christian into the real Body of Christ by the daily reception of Holy communion, the consecrated soul is permanently united with Christ unless of course the presence of mortal sin.

Thirdly and most importantly, when one is consecrated to the Holy Spirit one receives the necessary gifts so one can live a blameless life, holy and acceptable to the Triune God. The gifts of wisdom, understanding, knowledge, counsel, fortitude, piety and the fear of the Lord will inspire the consecrated soul to live a life most pleasing to God. The Holy Spirit will then makes His dwelling place and one will experience love, peace, joy, patience, kindness, faithfulness, gentleness and self control. Once one acquired His fruits the transformation begins and God's own life is conceived. It is the Holy Spirit that truly transform our Lady into the perfect likeness of her Groom. Once one is consecrated to the Holy Spirit it is most certain that He will never cease the works of the Father and the Son until the transformation is completed.

Our Lady made clear to her community that those who desires to be consecrated and dedicated to the Triune God should be done at Holy Mass so to receive that special singular grace from the Holy Spirit to live a perfect and holy life. Professed members of her community will dedicate itself serving the Catholic Church and the Order of our Lady of Unity.

Our Lady taught us the essentiality of replacing the old heaven so to establish the new heaven where the Triune God reigns also replacing the monotheistic God, there the beauty and glory of God tripled by the Beatific Vision and Glory of the Blessed Trinity. Indeed, the new heaven reserve for us is far more greater, more glorious and more beautiful than the old heaven and knowing this, Satan and the fallen angel's fury and wrath intensified against us. In his raging anger and jealousy Satan and his legion made their passion preventing us to reach the new heaven. They plotted to use all their powers to ruin and bring us down to hell.

But the Holy Spirit knew the dangers we are facing and that it takes more than living a good and blameless life to conquer the powerful Satanic forces vent in destroying our soul.

"And if the righteous scarcely be saved, where shall the ungodly and the sinner appear?" (1Peter 4:18).

In order to save many from the grasp of hell and Satan God quickly engineered that one must be incorporated to His own Body as the only solution in negating and neutralizing the power of hell and all the enemies of His church. And so, at the foot of the cross when Jesus our Lord expired, the old heaven was rent into oblivion and opening the new heaven.

Since her Son was consecrated as an Eternal Priest in the order of Melchisidek, He was the first one the holiest to enter the new heavens establishing the greatest kingdom for His Body still separated but with the greatest hope possessing it. As His only begotten Son, it was Jesus mission through His redeeming works to gather all into His Body establishing the one true church on earth where the new kingdom will stand and fight all of God's enemies.

The Gospel recorded that on the cross where her Son was still, a Roman soldier pierced His side with a lance where blood and water poured on the ground. Our Lady confirmed what St. John Chrysostom taught that the water and blood symbolized baptism and the Holy Eucharist. From these two sacraments holy Mother Church was born; from baptism, the cleansing water that gives rebirth and renewal through the Holy Spirit, and from the Eucharist. Since the symbol of baptism and the Eucharist flowed from His side that Christ fashioned the church, as He had fashioned Eve from the side of Adam. Moses gives a hint of this when he tells the story of the first man and makes him exclaim. Bone from my bones and flesh from my flesh! As God then took a rib from Adam's side to fashion a woman, so Christ has given us the Church. God took the rib when Adam, was in deep sleep, and in the same way Christ gave us the blood and water after His own death.

Our Lady saw at the foot of the cross that the water that came from her Son's sacred Body was the same water He promised to the woman of Samaria.

"But whosoever drinketh of this water that I shall give shall never thirst; but the water that I shall give him shall be in him a well of water springing up into everlasting life." (John 4:14).

Looking up to her Son a revelation was made to our Lady that sin can be conquered through our fusion to the Body of her Son. This is the reason why He had to build the Church for our own greatest benefit. Our incorporation to the Body of Christ make us truly one with God and such union makes us invincible and indestructible since we are under the protection of the One who conquered sin and death.

The death of her Son on the cross not only opened the new heaven but also renewed the phase of the earth where her Son established His kingdom of the new covenant where He reign as our King. He has come!!!

"I am He that liveth, and was dead; and, behold, I am alive for evermore, Amen! And have the keys of hell and death." (Revelation 1:18).

Our Lady's divine Son rose from the dead and now He is the king of glory and He is inviting all to become a member of His very own Body - the Church.

Before His death, Christ Jesus had already plan the establishment of His church as the only way we can ascend and enter the new heaven through the incorporation of God and man. It is only through one's membership to God's Body that one can be healed, one can be sanctified, one can be transformed into like Him. And after one's own death as part of God's Body it will also be resurrected and it will ascend to the new heaven where it will be welcome and embraced by God since it was and is His own Body.

"And I say also unto thee that thou art Peter, and upon this rock I will build my church; and the gates of hell shall not prevail against it." (Matthew 16:18).

Indeed, holy Mother Church is the only way one can enter the new heaven and all can see the daughter of God, the mother of God and the spouse of God is honored and venerated for she was and is always one with her Church - the Bride of her Son.

REFLECTION

"To the general assembly and church of the first born, which are written in heaven, and to God the judge of all, and to the spirits of just men made perfect." (Hebrews 12:23).

Holy Mother Church once establish became the vehicle to our sure salvation. Without the church God cannot save us. All the sins committed made us unacceptable to God. We have become so filthy and so ugly in His sight. If Satan is a terrifying sight to behold we too look worst than him. How can we return to God? Lots of prayers, penances, fasting, good works and offerings will not do. In the Old Testament God's people performed them all but heaven remained close. Who then can restore us to God?

None other than God Himself in His Second Persona. God the Father had become our enemy but because of love He found the perfect and only solution to our hopeless situation. He must now operate in a very unusual way by dividing Himself into three each one had that special specific function so everything will work to perfection. He needed His other two Persona because He cannot accept us into His kingdom in heaven without satisfying the horrible crimes continuously committed against God. Thus, the Messiah was needed to be the perfect sacrificial Lamb that can truly paid and justified all our sins in the past, present and future. After Christ our Lord died, the new heavens was wide opened ready and available to everyone but there was that hidden condition that all of must know in order we can enter and possess God and heaven. Wither you agree or not one must become integrated into the Body of the Eternal Priest Christ Jesus so we can be admitted to the new heaven. Without our enrollment in His church we are outside of His Body unprotected unsafe from all the enemies of our salvation. But integrated to the Body of Christ we received all the protection keeping us safe and secure from all the powerful assaults of our enemies. This is the only way we can survive and the surest way we can enter to the new heaven. Without the church and its powerful and potent sacraments we can not be born again. The existence of the church started by Peter commissioned by Christ is called Holy Mother Church where its members are first born through Christ our Lord. Holy Mother Church in its rite of baptism and confirmation certifies that one becomes the first born and our names are written in the Book of Life stored in the highest heaven. Holy Mother Church with Christ as Head will be the One who will justify, redeem and the Holy Spirit will work unceasingly until one is transform into God.

PRAYER

Holy Mary mother of the church pray for us that God's graces abundantly fall upon all His lost children that had fallen away separated from the real and true Body of Christ that they will come back to the one true church established by our Lord through His appointment of Peter as its visible head. Our Lady of Unity full of grace obtain from your beloved Son His powerful help by revealing Himself to every soul the necessity of their integration to His Church for the salvation of their soul. Amen.

CHAPTER NINE
· · · · · · · · · · · · · · · ·
WITH HER CHILDREN

At the foot of the cross, creation heard our Lord's voice to His sorrowful mother.

"Mother behold your son." God reminded our Lady the cost in redeeming us. The mother of God understood her calling. The Holy Spirit revealed to His spouse that much was given and much is required of her. She was enlightened that the Triune God greatly needed her full participation in completing His greatest works. We, the greatest works of His Hand can never be perfectly completed without the assistance of a lowly creature like Mary. Thus, Mary must receive all of God's grace so she can respond to the greatness of her calling otherwise His works will fail.

Our Lady did discerned that she must exercise all God's graces knowing there is a lot of works to be done in accomplishing His masterpiece. Let it be known that it is not in the world and its beauty nor the splendor of the universe nor the opening of the renovated heaven, nor the created seraphs and cherubim were His greatest creation. They are not. We are. She reminded us why her Son sacrifices everything because of us.

"When I see the heavens, the work of your hands, the moon and the stars you arranged, what is man that you should keep him in mind, mortal man, that you care for him?"

Indeed we are truly His masterpiece. We are created solely for Him and that is why God willingly gave up His Life for us.

"With glory and honor you crowned him."

Our Lady reminded us that we will received our greatest reward if we are obedient to His holy will. Once we conform our will to God's we will earn that glorious immortal crown of God's majesty and one will experience beyond our greatest and loftiest imagination and expectation. Paul simply described his own experience as no ears had heard or eyes had seen what is in store for those who love Him. Our Lady agreed that heaven and God cannot be described in words for by doing so we had done great injustice to the reward that awaits those who responded to the calling of holiness and perfection. Our Lady repeated what she told Bernadette at Lourdes that she cannot promise happiness here on earth but certainly she could on the next life.

Our Lady who received the greatest responsibility did fully participated to be His birthplace where God can enter into our humanity. She nourished and nurtured God's Son preparing the Messiah for His mission. And she fully participated in our redemption for what she had suffered and endured at the foot of the cross. She also knew that she must be fully active in dispensing all she received so all God's children will be save. Mary also understood what her divine Son meant when He said.

"Woman behold thy son." It is not only to be the mother of God but also all God's children. Knowing her calling our Lady intensified her involvement in helping and forming us to become one with God with our integration to the Body of her Son - the Church. We cannot be saved if we do not belong to His Body. We can never enter the new heavens unless our membership is confirmed and ratified by this one and only true church of which Christ is the Head and His mother is also the most powerful member.

Our Lady is also called mother of the church and rightly so for it was ordained that she and her children (members of His Body) are formed together. As there is only one God in three persons so does the one true church had three bodies but operating as one powerful force. The Church Militant marching toward the battlefield of good and evil. The Church Suffering where saved souls were in their final purifying process before its admittance to the new heaven. The Church Triumphant where the saved souls received their crown and eternally inducted as heirs of the Triune God. This three powerful body of the Catholic Church are so invincible that it can never be destroyed. But in his utter blindness Satan vowed to destroy this church that God Himself built but unfortunately for him our Lady is standing tall with her church.

"And I will put enmity between thee and the woman, and between thy seed and her said; it shall bruise thy head and thou shalt bruise his hill." (Genesis 3:15).

This was ordained by God that the war between the children of man and Satan will continue till the end of time. Thus the new earth became the first heaven where Satan continued his rebellion against God and His children. He could not accept the eviction and Satan will do everything in his power that we too cannot possess heaven. But our Lord and God knowing the great difficulties and obstacle we are facing lowered His kingdom in heaven by instructing Peter to establish the church where He will be the king and Christ reign will never end. In this church, are the potent powerful sacraments protecting preserving its members against all enemies of God but most of all it has the powerful protection of our Lady where Satan and his legions trembled with fear merely by the mention of her holy name.

It is the sons and daughters baptized and confirmed by the church that they are now the children of God and to our Lady. Satan will not stop seducing and stealing her children into his ledger but we are under her maternal care and protection.

The community were taught that our Lady is mother of all God's children for she is actually the coming of the second Eve. While the first Eve brought disobedience and destruction our Lady's obedience brought true life and graces to all her children.

Our Lady's children are classified as legitimate and the illegitimate. Obviously, those who were baptized and confirmed by holy mother church are our Lady's legitimate children while those who are not baptized and confirmed were the illegitimate ones. But not to offend anyone we are all God's children and we have everything to gain by being baptize and risking to lose everything if we do not.

"Mother behold they son."

It was Jesus who reminded His mother to look after His redeemed children and she did by utilizing all the graces she received from God. Millions became witnesses how the children of holy mother church received her help both corporally and spiritually. Mary's powerful intercession is as powerful as her own Son as shown by the miracle at Cana that if it is not God's time to perform His first miracle our Lady changed the will of God. All her legitimate children looked at her with such love and tenderness truly embracing her as its mother.

"Son behold your mother" It was the voice of Jesus reminding His Body, the church to never lose sight of a mother who will do everything in her power to help those who called on her. Let us remember how Mary changed the will of God.

"And when they wanted wine, the mother of Jesus said to Him, they have no wine." (John 2:3).

Just a hint from our Lady generated such powerful influence to the Triune God.

We can also learned from the wedding at Cana is full of symbolism of our own future wedding to God. However, one must belong to His Body otherwise there is no marriage. This is the greatest reason why Jesus came into our world not only to redeem us but to gather and draw us into His Own Body (church) and our integration made us a part of God. When man and woman become one its union brought another life. And when Jesus is one with His church its union brought Christians into the world.

God willed that our Lady will have the greatest role in the formation of the first church. She was enthrone queen of heaven and earth and every Catholic Church throughout the earth honored Mary as mother of the church. Blessed statues and images of her inside the church attracts and draws devout Catholics seeking her help and powerful intercession of their needs. She listened joyfully to the unending voices vocal and silent Holy Rosary prayer:

"Hail Mary full of grace. The Lord is with you. Blessed are you among women and blessed is the fruit of your womb Jesus. Holy Mary mother of God pray for us sinners now and at the hour of our death. Amen."

After the Holy Mass and the Our Father, the Holy Rosary is one powerful and most effective prayer of the church that will bring positive and blessed results. If anyone wants confirmation of how powerful is our Lady's intercession one will be shock for the endless list of witnesses with how our Lady obtained all kinds of signal graces.

Just observe how Jesus was troubled and affected when Mary hinted that there is no more wine for the guests of the wedding at Cana. Can you ever imagine that our God will be bothered and affected by a mere creature made of dust?

"Jesus said unto her, woman, what I have to do with thee? Mine hour is not yet come?" (John 2:4).

He knew that His mission here on earth was to do His Father's will. But this woman touched Him like no other creature by altering God's agenda in performing His first miracle - water to wine. Although it was not the appointed time to do so Jesus had to performed. At this wedding

He was not supposed to show what He can do but the power of this woman bothered and affected Him. God allowed such event so we can see the greatness of Mary's intercessory power. But it also showed us that God will always provide what we need. Wine was truly needed for this is what a wedding celebration must have a joyous occasion and there should be wine available at all times. But they run out. Mary knew that God will always provide for what was truly needed in everyone's life. Being God Himself Jesus must do something so the wedding celebration will be joyful and cheerful. For wine always cheer a man's heart. There is truly a need that it had to be provided and with the presence of God and His mother collusively agreed that Jesus must act to provide even though against His will.

"His mother saith unto the servants whatever He saith with you, do it." (John 2:5).

The wedding at Cana is one of the greatest scene in the new testament showing us the importance of the establishment of God's one and only true church. It was Jesus first miracle and there is that deep hidden mystery of how the church truly save creation. The changing of water into wine symbolizes our baptism integrating us into God's Body. Once we became a member of the Body of Christ (Church) we are to celebrate joyfully our own mystical wedding. Thus, the church is born. And the Holy Mass became one of the greatest gift we receive from God where wine is offered by human hands presented and placed at the altar with the Holy Spirit waiting for the priest voice saying (This is my Blood) and much liked His overshadowing Mary, He will be the One who will change wine into the real Blood of Christ as to continue the un bloody shedding of the Lamb of God perpetuated by the Eternal Priesthood of Christ.

"The next day John seeth Jesus coming unto him, and saith, Behold the Lamb of God, which taketh away the sins of thew world." (St John 1:29).

The word of John the Baptist was fulfilled seeing Jesus coming up to him at the Jordan river so he can be baptized. But wait, God himself had to be baptized? No, it was God making water as an instrument for enrollment to those who wants to follow Him. And because He is the Head of the church He too must participate in this sacred enrollment for He is the greatest part of that Body.

And in this one and true church, our Lady was ordained by God to be our mother. And those who are baptized and confirmed by the Catholic Church are called the legitimate children of God.

Those who are not members of His Body are called our Lady's illegitimate children and even though they do not care much help and assistance our Lady through her church never stop in reaching out for them so they will know the fullness of truth. The church and her children never stop their mission in spreading the gospel and even though numbers were not recorded there are so many Mary's illegitimate children being converted everyday to Catholicism making them her legitimate children.

Thus the new earth did replaced the old earth by the establishment of God's one and only true church where its members can now be in heaven even though still in earthly exile courtesy of their Head who is seated at the right hand of the Father continuously interceding for His Body still a work in progress and being form by the Holy Spirit until the final finish transformation completed.

What a mighty difference does the establishment of His Church. The coming down of God in His Second Identity as Redeemer uniting itself to His creation so this unique divine interference will permanently cement us and we will never be separated from Him. But of course, sin does. What made this church powerful and invincible was the real true Presence of God in the Blessed Sacrament disguised as a tiny Host making Himself available at all times where the truly faithful believers can come converse, console, worship and adore Jesus where abundant blessings and graces are acquired. When He ascended to His father in heaven as promised He sent us His Third Persona the Holy Spirit as the necessary reinforcement providing potent powers so we can always united with Him. God remembered how His chosen people went haywire when Moses their spiritual leader went up the mountain for forty days and nights and thinking he was not coming back they made their own choice to create and made their own gods. Based from what happened to them, our God the greatest genius there is then made sure we will not make the same mistake. Thus, Jesus did accomplished many things for our sake and we should take advantage all He gave us.

We who belong to the Catholic Church is in solid foundation not on sandy sand and it is our Lady never compromising that all her children does come and be a part of this powerful religious machinery for Holy Mother Church was, is and will be always one with the Triune God.

And standing with Him is our Lady with all God's graces ready and always available for dispensing for all her children legitimate or not for any child is in the greatest need of its mother. Our Lady of Unity is waiting.

REFLECTION

"Ye are of God, little children, and have overcome them; because greater is he that is in you, than he that is in the world." (1John 4:4).

As Mary brought Jesus into the world perpetually establishing His Presence so to draw and gather God's children into His Own Body coming our adoption permanently legal making us real and truly heirs of His majestic glorious kingdom. In truth and reality, we can never be worthy to be called His children for God is God and we are only made of dust. But all praises and eternal thanksgiving to His Son by purchasing us with His very own life and by His Blood and Water poured on the earth became the seed which sprung into existence Holy Mother Church making possible our adoption as God's children. But are we really appreciating what our Lord Jesus did for us? From what we saw in this world so very few truly appreciate and placed the greatest value for His marvelous and amazing works. We are no longer children of darkness as John said but rather children of light. Are we justly and rightly giving God what is due Him? We never did. But, Holy Mother Church whom God's only begotten Son is the Head and our Lady of Unity as its prominent powerful member justly and rightly glorifies and honor Him to its highest degree. And it is our greatest loss and risk not to be incorporated in God's Body. A small unprofitable business enterprise if merged to the most wealthiest corporation will be benefited greatly from the merger. The same principle applies if one becomes a member of the Catholic Church. Billions will not agree but truth is truth. By being baptized and confirmed by the church one truly and really becomes a legitimate child inheriting all the wealth and treasure of the Catholic Church.

PRAYER

Hail holy mother of God, on the cross Jesus your Son ordained you to be our mother also. Pray for us sinners children of darkness enslaved by the enemies of our salvation quickly in your great love and mercy assist us your afflicted children with the treasury of God's graces entrusted to you that we will be truly converted to become children of light so we can inherit His promised kingdom where we will love, praise and adore Him for all of eternity. Amen

CHAPTER TEN
· ·
WITH HER FRUITS

"A good tree cannot bring forth evil fruit, neither can a corrupt tree bring forth good fruit. " (Matthew 7:18).

The garden of Eden was filled with all kinds of trees providing Adam and Eve with a variety of delicious fruits. One tree and its fruit was forbidden. As we all know, they did eat the fruit of the tree and the rest was our history. The fruit of that tree did give us knowledge of good and evil. And it also put a curse on us. Did that tree bears good or bad fruit? Both. The fruit of that forbidden tree give us both the good and the bad in our existence. By eating the forbidden fruit we were evicted from paradise which sounded bad since we lost the friendship of God and also losing our immortality but in reality there is that greater good awaiting for us.

Indeed our greatest good was the coming of God in the flesh retrieving His greatest work and restoring us to His friendship. God did not restrain Adam and Eve from eating the forbidden fruit for it was His plan that the garden of Eden was not the perfect place for His children. God had prepared the new heaven which is the far greater than the old for there He will share everything to us. But to do so it will greatly cost us so much and also God's own life. This is our challenge. In the tree of our life what kind of fruit can we produce? The choice is simply our own as to what can we bring into the garden of God. Two models are presented to us. Eve and Mary. Eve was the mother of all creation for without her womb there was no creation. She was called to be the perfect companion for Adam in His garden but instead of helping her husband she made him disobeyed God which brought forth disaster, diseases, death and destruction to her children. Mary, on the other hand chose to do God's will by bearing the blessed fruit in her womb. Our Lady brought hope of eternal life of happiness and above all she brought God to us. It was the fruit that comes from the womb of Mary which changes the complexion of our miserable and hopeless existence. She gave us back our God whom Eve lost. Without Jesus we are more miserable that the animals with no hope at all to possess eternal life of unending joy and happiness.

"Hail Mary full of grace. The Lord is with you. Blessed are you among women and blessed is the fruit of the womb Jesus."

The second most powerful prayer of the church after the Our Father is the Holy Rosary. After professing our Christian faith, the Our Father follows and then the Hail Mary's. Our Lady's prayer should always be together with the perfect prayer taught by Jesus. It is fitting to do so since our Lady is always united with the Holy Trinity and so the church did the most holy thing in propagating the Holy Rosary of our Lady.

Even though the offsprings of the church labelled as Protestants kept criticizing their mother church of idolatry for having statues of the Blessed Virgin Mary and for the repetitive prayers of the Holy Rosary have no negative effect on the devout and faithful Catholic. Simply, Protestants are clueless how Mary's powerful maternal intercession have resulted in countless miracles. All the miracles recorded in Sacred Scriptures paled in comparison to what Mary procured from God. Unfortunately, the whole world had no clue how the sons and daughters of the Catholic Church canonized as Saints performed thousands and thousands of amazing miracles as a sign that this church was and is the only one true church for all God's children. Such incredible miracles was made possible because they have both Jesus and Mary. The church knew and recognized how powerful are Mary's prayers and how quickly God responded to her as shown at the wedding at Cana.

Every creature on earth should revere and honor this greatest lady of our own race for she produced the fruit that save God's creation. Without our Lady there is no salvation. Without her fruit God's mercy cannot be granted for only Jesus her Son can plead and obtain us mercy.

Obviously, the greatest fruit in our Lady's womb was none other but the Messiah foretold by the prophets of old as the Redeemer and Savior of humanity. He will come representing His Father to make peace so we can be restored to God. Finally, God in our very own flesh will show us how to love perfectly bringing hope to humanity consumed by darkness and death.

"For God so loved the world that He gave his only begotten son, that whosoever believeth in him should not perish, but have everlasting life." (John 3:16).

Our Lady coined this immortal word into the heart and soul of John for he was chosen to prepare the world for the coming Savior who will be our everlasting guide to the new heavens. God had come in the flesh to be seen so we may believe that He truly exist. For only in our flesh we will be able to see Him for no one can stand the reality of His Being. Our Lord had chosen His cousin, John the Baptist, to be the merging agent uniting the old covenant with the new thus replacing the first earth with His new earth.

Before John was conceived, his mother who was the cousin of Mary received their heavenly Guest as our Lady came to visit and serve Elizabeth.

"And entered into the house of Zachariahs, and saluted Elizabeth." (Luke 1:40).

Our Lady joyfully informed her cousin that the Lord had chosen her and salvation came to Elizabeth and her household. Mary's presence and God's enlightened Elizabeth and she was overwhelmed with joy. At the sound of our Lady's voice Elizabeth was enlightened interiorly that truly Mary was carrying and bringing God to their home. She was filled with the Holy Spirit which overwhelmed her spiritually and emotionally that John who was still in Elizabeth's womb leaped with joy knowing that his Lord and His mother came which humbled them. Just like what our Lady felt when she was presented to her Eternal Father, John experienced what it is like to be in God's Presence. The Holy Spirit which filled Elizabeth with joy also filled the greatest prophet.

Even before this blessed meeting, God formed John in her mother's barren womb with divine Light receiving the gifts of the Holy Spirit and his life was all for God alone earning praise from Jesus. Much like her son, Elizabeth was also chosen to be our Lady's prophet so the whole world and all generation to come will know who our Lady truly is.

"Blessed art thou among women and blessed is the fruit of thy womb. And whence is this to me, that the mother of my Lord should come to me? For behold as soon as thy voice of thy salutation sounded in my ears, the infant in my womb leaped for joy, and blessed art thou, that has believed, because this things shall be accomplished that were spoken to thee by the Lord."

Elizabeth understood like no other creature the noblest and most highest privileges our Lady received from God. Truly she is the mother of God She is the pride of the human race and also God's pride knowing such masterpiece came from His holy Hands. Having received the highest honor and glory from His Creator our Lady was filled with God and announced the greatness and goodness of God.

"My soul doth magnify the Lord and my spirit hath rejoiced in God my Savior. Because He hath regarded the humility of His handmaid; for behold from henceforth all generations shall call me blessed. Because He that is mighty hath done great things to me; and holy is His name. And in His mercy is from generation unto generation to them that fear Him. He hath showed might in his arm; He hath scattered the proud in the conceit of their heart. He hath put down the mighty from their seat and exalted the humble. He hath filled the hungry with good things; and the rich he hath sent empty away. He hath received Israel, his servant, being mindful of His mercy; As He spoke to our fathers, to Abraham and His seed forever."

Our Lady's canticle was the fruit of her great love for God and us. She wants us to recite it to remind ourselves that we too who were specially created by God to become like Him can rise beyond ourselves by imitating our Lady's life and love for God. It was the Holy Spirit, her Spouse that taught her the canticle so she can share to her children and to her Church. This is the canticle that all of us must recite in humble prayer to God and according to her revelation to the community that He will be pleased to those who faithfully prayed the canticle before retiring to bed. Mary's canticle is a powerful meditation elevating the soul to the state of contemplation and one will understand why her praises to God is also our very own.

"My soul proclaims the greatness of the Lord."

Mary did fathomed who God is and her knowledge of Him was so overwhelming that if we are in her shoes our proclamation of His greatness will resound to the ends of the earth and to the end of time. But our knowledge of Him is so limited and we barely scratch the surface of His greatness. Only those who give Him the greatest of love can fathom who God is. And His greatness.

"My spirit rejoices in God my Savior for He has looked with favor on His lowly servant."

Mary's exceeding joy cannot be contained for what God had done to her. She was only a speck of dust yet she received the greatest favor ever to all His creation and that was the fullness of grace. Even the powerful angels only received little compared to what our Lady received from God. All the saints past present and future lumped together also received little compared to what Mary received. Like her, we too are made of dust but we can also receive the fullness of God by simply imitating our Lady's life to perfection.

"From this day all generations will call me blessed."

Indeed, Holy Mother Church rightfully called her as the Blessed Virgin Mary and children of the church embraced, revered and honored her as blessed among women. But even more blessed was that womb that formed and delivered to us the Prince of Peace where the human race can now be reconciled to their lost God. Our Lady of Unity as prophesied will be the one who will unite all His children to the Triune God.

"The Almighty has done great things for me, and holy is His Name."

Mary's gratitude penetrated the highest heaven because of her greatest reverence and appreciation to the Holy One who chose her as His greatest instrument in fulfilling His marvelous works. She revealed that each one of us is also chosen like her if only we also chose Him by our full cooperation of His will.

"He has mercy on those who fear Him in every generation."

Mary's love for God was nourished and nurtured with reverential fear of never offending or displeasing the One who loves her greatly. And it was the mercy of God that she received all His graces. From Adam to Noah to Abraham to Isaac, to Jacob, to Moses, to John and to all the saints in heaven received God's mercy. Salvation is only possible if we seek His mercy. Otherwise, there is no salvation if one does not repent, seek His mercy and truly be converted by diligently striving to sin no more.

"He has shown the strength of His arm, he has scattered the proud in their conceit."

Mary knew how powerful is God and nothing can stand against Him. Those who opposes God should recall how the mighty army of Egypt were destroyed. We should remember how the powerful Lucifer and his legions were easily casted down by the power of His Name, "Who is like God". Michael, the archangel proclaimed in his name who God is. Let us never oppose His holy will and always cultivate that reverential fear never at all cost to offend or displease our good and Holy God. With all fervor always strive to acquire the highest virtue of humility if one desires to be exalted by God. God despises the proud and the conceited and we should always remind ourselves that we had nothing at all to be proud.

"He has cast down the mighty from their throne and has lifted up the lowly."

Reinforcing that humility is the greatest virtue that all of us should strive to acquire and whatever position, talent or power gifted to us always to acknowledged that it belongs to God and we should strive the very best to use them only for God's greatest glory and honor. We should avoid at all cost never to think that we are better than anyone else. To do so we have imitated Lucifer.

We should imitate the lowliness of our Lady.

"He has lifted the hungry with good things, and the rich he sent away empty."

Mary's greatest hunger and thirst for God was one of the reason why she was chosen to participate in God's greatest work. Although ordained, her holy heritage flowed in her being that burning hunger and thirst for God always enflaming her heart with the greatest love for Him. Knowing the greatness of her love for Him, God who cannot be outdone in generosity then returned the favor by giving her the fullness of His grace. If we imitate her by desiring God above anything else then He will also return the greatest favor. But if we lack the desire to possess and please God we receive nothing but the emptiness that will always be in our heart and soul.

"He has come to the help of His servant Israel for he has remembered the promise He made to our fathers, to Abraham and his children for ever."

When it seems that hopelessness and helplessness will be our lot forever God as promised came down from His throne in heaven to fulfill the prophecies that He will save those who seek His mercy. With Mary's yes, God had finally came to help creation bringing us the blessed hope where we will be able to enter His promised kingdom prepared to those who love Him. Such opportunity was for all.

Our Lady was the greatest tree in God's garden unlike the forbidden fruit in the garden of Eden. Mary's fruit brought hope and the reality of possessing that lost immortality and to obtain that eternal life of unending joy and indescribable happiness that is freely offered to the world. Mary not only gave us God and heaven but most importantly our Lady and mother will bring us back to God. If and only if you let her help you.

REFLECTION

"For the fruit of the Spirit is in all goodness and righteousness and truth." Ephesians 5:9.

In God's garden sprung the greatest tree and Mary brought the greatest fruit which God could not have done Himself. The fruit of her womb unites God and man. Truly Mary was indeed blessed among women for without her womb God's divine seed cannot be sowed and the true tree of Life cannot sprout and it could not be planted on earth. Without the Messiah, Holy Mother Church cannot exist and there will be no hope for us all. The Catholic Church was also Mary's greatest fruit.

Our Lady was the greatest tree and truly full of God because though a woman by nature became in reality and truth God's mother. Baffling but truth. What do we call someone who carry in her womb and deliver it as a living child.? Mother!!! And Mary is truly the mother of God and her fruit was Might, Power, Peace, Beauty, Truth, Splendor, Supreme and Sovereignty.

But what are we going to do for her? What kind of gifts shall we offer her? She is the mother of God!!! Could we at the very least return some reverence and respect? We greatly owed her our love and praise. As God children we have to honor her for she was the mother of our salvation. Not to honor her clearly dishonored not only the Son but also the Father and the Holy Spirit. As scripture commanded us, honor thy father and mother. If we greatly honored God the Father what about our mother?

If we truly want our salvation then it is truly wise and just to make the mother of God as the other most powerful force in helping us to reach our heavenly homeland.

PRAYER

Mother of God blessed is your womb that brought us our salvation. Blessed be God in His Three Divine Person for giving us a mother who will never stop in helping us in all our corporal and spiritual needs. As you helped in bringing us Jesus our Savior assists us O Mother of Perpetual Help by bringing us to your Divine Son and obtain from the Lord of Mercy pardon for all of our crimes and iniquities and the grace of conversion that will truly lead us in following Him by carrying our cross and denying ourselves from all that displeased Him. Our Lady of Unity, full of grace pray for us. Amen.

CHAPTER ELEVEN
. . . .
WITH HER ENEMIES

"And I will put enmity between thee and the woman, and between thy seed and her seed; it shall bruise thy head, and thou shalt bruise his heel." (Genesis 3:15).

God ordained that we the children of Eve will be at war against Satan and his followers till the end of time. Once Lucifer was evicted from heaven his anger towards God will be forever knowing he cannot do anything against God, Lucifer or Satan channeled his rage towards us. Satan blamed us for his downfall because of his extreme jealousy that we, made of dust, will be made heirs of God's kingdom instead of him. In his raging anger and hatred Satan vowed he will do everything in his power to prevent us from inheriting the greatest kingdom one will ever imagine. Such raging passion made Satan and his legions roamed all over the world deceiving and tricking us so we can never possessed heaven. Indeed, it is true that we do not deserve to be in heaven because we kept offending and rebelling against God while Lucifer made only one mistake by over ambitious desire to replace God. Satan thought that grave injustice were done to him and his followers by choosing us instead of them. They could not accept that we are destined to become like God. How could we ever deserve heaven with the way we treated our God. But they have no idea that God Himself will correct all our wrongs by making good our bad by making right all our wrong and they have no idea that it is the Triune God that will transform and make us like Him. Yes, God will make every thing perfect through His involvement by integrating imperfect humanity into His perfection. And God will enter into our humanity through a woman. Satan became more furious knowing God will be conceived in the lowest of creature, through a weak woman. But they were clueless that this simple woman have all of God's power.

"And there appeared a great wonder in heaven; a woman clothed with the sun and the moon under her feet, and upon her head a crown of twelve starts." (Revelation 12:1).

The fallen angels despite their superior mind and intellect could not figure out why this woman was wearing a crown with twelve stars. Our Lady's enthronement was prophesied by God's beloved disciple that she will be greatly exalted and the whole world will see her glorious majesty towering over the moon and the cosmos. Like her Son's transfiguration at Mount Tabor our Lady's own transfiguration is as glorious for she was filled with the brilliance of the sun.

"And as he prayed, the fashion of his countenance was altered, and his raiment was white and glistening." (Luke 8:29).

Once known to the fallen angels that this same woman who will bear God's only begotten Son quickly sought our Lady's whereabout believing that they can stop her fulfilling God's plan.

"And when the dragon saw that he was cast unto the earth, he persecuted the woman which brought forth the man child." (Revelation 12:13).

The fallen angels knew that this woman will be God's most important worker in accomplishing God's greatest works. Satan and his legions were vent on destroying her by unleashing all their power against her and the holy Infant Child.

"And the serpent cast out of his mouth water as flood after the woman that he might cause her to be carried away of the flood." (Revelation 12:15).

But the fallen angels were deceiving themselves that they can destroy her and the child refusing to acknowledge that their power were not like God. In their pride and arrogance they were blinded that they are more powerful than God who made them. An angel of darkness cannot distinguish what is truth and what is not.

"And the earth helped the woman, and the earth opened her mouth, and swallowed up the flood which the dragon cast out from his mouth." (Revelation 12:16).

Thus the fallen angels were powerless in their attempt to prevent God with His plans. And after their failure they kept on pursuing their plans in destroying our Lady for she had became their greatest enemy. They also knew they will be our greatest helper. Since they could not do anything against their Maker they were unleashing their fury and rage against

Mary knowing that she will bear the Messiah who will be our light and salvation. Satan and his legions were so preoccupied that they were on her shadow. They keep following her trying to find an opening where they can execute their power against this woman a descendant of that weak woman named Eve. If Satan was able to tricked her in tempting Adam her husband, they also believed that they can easily deceive and trick this very innocent girl named Mary. So they went after Joseph thinking he was an easy prey like Adam.

"Then Joseph her husband, being a just man, and not willing to make her a pub-lick example, was minded to put her away privily." (Matthew 1:19).

It was Lucifer's legion who clouded Joseph's mind that Mary was not good enough to be his wife. Maliciously, Satan falsely accused Mary as being unfaithful and suggested to Joseph should present her to the community about her infidelities. To do so, Mary would be stone to death ending also the life of her Child. As Joseph was deeply troubled, Satan can taste victory but———

"But while he thought on these things, behold, the angel of the Lord appeared unto him in a dream saying, Joseph, thou son of David, fear not to take unto thee Mary thy wife; for that which is conceived in her is of the Holy Ghost." (Matthew 1:20).

By God's grace, the angel came and enlightened Joseph not to take the devil's suggestion and being a holy man he was able to discern what is God's will.

With her enemies defeat, they became more enraged and more determined to destroy this woman and Child. Then came another event where her enemies saw another opportunity to destroy Mary and the Child.

"When Herod the king had heard these things, he was troubled, and all Jerusalem with him" (Matthew 2:3).

It was widely known of the prophecy of the coming birth of the king of the Jews draw nearer which tormented Herod and without the grace of God, it was not difficult for Satan to tempt him that the only way his kingship prevails was to seek and slew the child. They kept on working on Herod's pride which promptly ordered that every newborn child be killed.

"Then Herod, when he saw that he was mocked of the wise men, was exceedingly wroth, and sent forth, and slew all the children that were on Bethlehem, and in all the coasts, thereof from two years old and under, according to the time which he had diligently inquired of the wise men." (Matthew 2:16).

Again, Satan's evil plot failed when God intervened through His angel.

"And when they were departed, behold the angel of the Lord appeared to Joseph in a dream, saying, Arise, and take the young child and his mother, and flee into Egypt, and, be thou there until I bring thee word; For Herod will seek the young child to destroy him." (Matthew 2:13).

It was not surprising why Joseph is revered and honored as the most powerful saint second only to Mary for he too was always perfect in doing God's will. Joseph was God's perfect choice to be husband to His beloved daughter and also guardian of His only begotten Son, Jesus. In Sacred Scripture, Joseph spoke no single word but his action were so decisive and dramatic in defending and defeating God's powerful enemy through his obedience to God's messenger. The church had no doubt that Joseph also played a major role in our salvation for he was the head of the holy family. He protected and preserved Mary and Jesus.

In recognition to Joseph, the Queen of heaven and earth sweetly told him.

"My husband and my master, if we have received from the hands of the Most High such great blessings of grace it is meet that we joyfully accept temporal afflictions. We bear with us the Creator of heaven and earth; if He had placed us so near to Him, what arms shall be able to harm us, even if it be the arm of Herod? Wherever we carry with us all our good, the highest treasure of heaven, our Lord, our guide and true light, there can be no desert; but He is our rest, our portion, and our country. All these goods we possess in having His company; let us proceed to fulfill His will."

Despite all the powers of Satan and his legions they simply cannot stop Mary in giving us God in the flesh. It was God's most holy will that creation will be able to finally see what had been promised so long ago. Sensing that they could never harm or destroy our Lady and the Child, Satan unleashed their frustration and anger towards us. Of course, many were victimized with Satan shackling them into the slavery of sin. They easily fell to Satan simply because they were unprotected for they have lived their lives godless. They did not conform to God's will and Satan need not use his power to enslaved them.

With the war unending the fallen angels were not going out easy even though they kept failing in destroying our Lady and her Child. Refusing to go down in defeat, Satan changed strategy since he was powerless against our Lady and instead shifted into a different direction by going after His less protected Creation whose way of life were repulsive and displeasing to God. They also went after those whose faith were weak. They went after other religious leaders whose primary motive was not really to serve God but themselves. Satan assisted greatly their ministry attracting and drawing many souls so they became victimized by these false shepherds whose master was the prince of lies. Thus, with all their might and forces they spent all their time roaming around the world never stop seeking the ruins of souls. They claimed victory knowing that so very few souls were able to enter the new heaven and they were rejoicing with their abundant harvest. They celebrated that they have taken away from God what belongs to Him.

However, the master of lies, Satan was enraged once he found out that what he thought was an abundant harvest of souls bound for hell was not so. Satan was tormented foaming with rage that more than half of those souls were not delivered to him and he could not figure out what happened to them since they were not admitted to the new heaven. Finally after their frantic searched they discovered those souls supposedly belonging to him were detained in another place where he was powerless claiming them.

Where are your justice? You are not playing fair with us. You took away that was ours. Those sinful souls were mine and in your perfect justice those souls should be in hell. You knew their sins and they do not deserve to be in the new heaven. Satan's complained was heard but God was silent. He was baffled and became very restless and they spent all their time and power to find where they are. Finally they did.

Purgatory. This was the place where Satan found out where multitude of souls were detained. He was confused why they were not delivered into hell when he knew they were all stained with sin and imperfection. But Satan had no idea that it was our Lady who had the greatest influenced in the establishment of purgatory depriving Satan's abundant harvest of souls. The souls detained in purgatory were saved from hell because of the tremendous powerful intercession of Our Lady of Grace. She was pleading with tears in her eyes that such a place was necessary and essential to spare so many souls going to hell. She pleaded to the most Holy Trinity that without purgatory so very few can enter into the new heaven and this mystical place must become an integral part of the Catholic Church. Our Lady's pleading was presented to the highest court and assembly in heaven where the Triune God have

75

no choice but to consider knowing she was greatly privilege with the fullness of their grace. Full of wisdom, she pleaded that if a holy person is liable to fall at least seven times a day what are the chances of all His children devoid of holiness? Of course, God had already conceived the idea since to enter the new heaven one had to be perfectly purified and completely cleansed that no speck of stain remained in the soul. And the establishment of the Church Suffering was perfectly justifiable knowing that all of us could never get rid of sin and not having purgatory heaven will be deserted. By doing so, God will be greatly glorified with so many multitude of souls surrounding His throne singing and praising their merciful and loving Father.

The existence of purgatory brought Satan and his followers to their greatest defeat. They worked hard harvesting those souls and had even celebrated their great victory but they were more enraged with their latest defeat. They were more enraged to our Lady knowing she was responsible for their failures. Even though billions and more will not believe in the existence of Purgatory, Holy Mother Church embraced the dogma based on the logic that God is so pure and holy and we are not. Who of us can truly believe or claim that we are like God?

Or who among us can stand before His holy Presence face to face? No one.

If the heavens trembled at His presence, we, made of dust will disintegrate into the tiniest particle. Before we can become truly worthy of being one with Him in heaven perfect purification is needed.

Our Lady knew why she pleaded for its existence knowing how difficult and demanding is our journey to the new heavens and impossible for us to be completely transformed into God that if purgatory is not available then so very few can get in that they can be counted with our fingers. Our Lady knew that nothing defiled nothing impure but only the truly perfect and holy are worthy but even so must passed but briefly in God's purifying fire of love. She also revealed to the community that divine justice must be fully satisfied for it was His will that for every word and deed had to be accounted for. And all of us failed miserably such standard and it is only in purgatory that we can justly pay the last penny we owed. With so many unbelievers about purgatory, it was revealed by our Lady inspiring Paul to teach Holy Mother Church of the divine concept of our purgation that we all need different degree of purification.

"If different ones build on this foundation (of Christ) with gold, silver, precious stones, wood, hay or straw, the work of each will be made clear. The day will disclose it. That day will make its appearance with fire, and fire will test the quality of each man's work. If the building a man has raised on this foundation still stands he will receive his recompense; if a man's building burns, he will suffer loss. He himself will be saved, but only as one fleeing through fire." (1Corinthians 3:12).

With Paul's teaching, how could anyone missed this beautiful and magnificent concept which basically was for our very own greatest good? One need not to be a great theologian that indeed Paul was referring to purgatory.

As mother of the church, our Lady of Sorrows made sure that the Church Militant offers Holy Masses continuously for the suffering souls in purgatory so they will received consolation and even released from this beautiful prison of God's marvelous love. She instructed faithful Catholics to habitually and regularly offered Holy Mass for them so both sides will reap benefits. Martin Luther, a monk and priest revolted to such concept of purgation specially when he accused the church of selling indulgences for the souls in purgatory. He was inspired by Satan and the Catholic church was devastated where millions followed Luther by separating themselves from the one and only true church. Luther splintered Holy Mother Church because he was so displeased with the idea of selling indulgences but such practices were exercised even before the church was built.

"He took up a collection with a view to the splendid reward that awaits those who had gone to rest in godliness. He made atonement for the dead that they might be freed from sin." (2Maccabees 12:43-46).

As mother of salvation and mother of all souls our Lady worked the hardest and the longest in collusion with Holy Mother Church so that many more souls will be save and she indeed had defeated her enemies simply of the fullness of God's grace. Thus, all enemies of Mary, our Lady of Grace will never have any chance of all against the mother of God.

REFLECTION

"But if thou shalt indeed obey his voice, and do all that I speak; then I will be an enemy unto thine enemies, and an adversary unto thine adversaries"(Exodus 23:22).

Like her Son, Mary's obedience to God was perfect at all times. She never said no to her God. In all of God's creation nothing will ever equal nor surpass Mary's perfect obedience that once she heard the message of Gabriel she promptly obeyed what was God's will. Satan and his legions are powerless against this great Lady for God was fully with her. They tried to deceive themselves that Mary was simply like Eve and they can easily and quickly lured her in obeying them so they can led to her destruction. They never stop trying to destroy her but only finding failures upon failures that made them even more miserable. We may recall that those who blest Israel will be blest by God and those who cursed Israel will be cursed by God. But Mary was far more greater than Israel and we should be very careful not to become Mary's enemy. If we do, we made war against God simply because she is the mother of God. We should be very careful not to become an enemy of the Catholic Church because Mary is a part of it and most importantly she is the mother of the church. The Papacy as its visible leader had been attacked and abused throughout its reign as Vicar of Christ but its leadership never responded knowing our Lady will be the one who will protect and defend the church. And curses it will be upon those who kept attacking and mocking the Catholic Church and worst they have become God's worst enemy. Our Lady loves all God's creation even her enemies that hated or despised her.

PRAYER

Our Lady of Unity be with us always knowing the perilous journey we have to take entering the narrow path to eternal life. We humbly beseech you O mother of God, full of grace, to obtain for us the special grace that you will never permit us to be separated from your maternal care knowing that those who are under your constant care and protection will never be lost. O holy Mary, protect us from all our enemies for we are but weak sinners susceptible to worldly allurements and pleasures, from the assaults and lies of the devil and from our very own sinful nature. Trusting always in your love and sweetness we place ourselves in your motherly protection. Amen.

CHAPTER TWELVE
· ·
WITH HER MILITANT CHURCH

As the Bride and Body of Christ, the church have three mystical member but always one with Him. Much like the Three Persons of God, each had a specific important function to make perfect His works.

Our Lady revealed to the community the essentiality and the necessity that the one true God of Noah, Abraham, Isaac and Jacob must become three simply because a monotheistic God could not possibly accomplished in transforming dust into divinity. It was revealed to us that the Three Persons of God should become a reality for it is the only way we can become like Him. Our Lady had the complete knowledge of His Three Persona for she alone had the most intimate relation where she experienced perfect union with the Triune God. There is no theologian nor spiritual master or guru that can fathom this great unfathomable mystery of the Trinitarian God.

She simply explained that God the Father cannot create some one to become like Him despite His omnipotence and might. He cannot create Himself for God was and is not created but existed. He did created the angels who were perfect spirits but they cannot become like God. God created them to serve Him but we are created to become like Him. This is the greatness of our being that we should always be mindful of this truth and we should never compromise our existence by taking for granted what God had done for us. Our Lady knew why the process of transforming His creation into like Him takes more than His Oneness and there was the need of His other Two Persona although distinct but the same one God. She informed the community how awesome was God's plan for each one of us and how great is our destiny to be transform into God. Even the pure angels envied us for they also knew how marvelous God's plan was. And so, the First Person cannot be Mary's spouse for He was her Father therefor the Holy Spirit will be the Third Persona who will be her Spouse.

"And the angel answered and said unto her the Holy Ghost shall come upon thee, and the power of the Highest shall overshadow thee; therefore also the holy thing which shall be born of thee shall be called the Son of God." (Luke 1:35).

Without the Third Persona, the Messiah will not exist as God man thus the plan of God cannot be accomplished. But with His Third Persona, our Lady became His spouse where the conception of the Messiah was made possible by this holy union. Though we are created, the conception of Jesus in her womb was an act of uniting God's creation (humanity) to Himself (divinity) thus with this unique union God and man will never be separated again. This is the new covenant deleting everything in the past where God and man were always in enmity with each other. In the old covenant, God was constantly challenged and provoked by His chosen people despite witnessing all His great miracles and despite of the Mosaic law as their guide, the war between Creator and creation continued with no peace in sight. It was then that God's Third Persona must enter into the womb of a creature where humanity and divinity became one where the Prince of Peace made a silent entrance to our world. Indeed, peace had finally come between God and man. The new heaven will also be opened once Christ Jesus accomplished everything His Father asked him to do. With the birth of God in Mary's womb, heaven was lowered so we will be able to see and know intimately the invisible unreachable God who loves us. This was the greatest moment of our history the birth of God on the land of our exile. By His coming God will be actively involved in making sure we get it through His teachings and example so we can be with Him to God's promised eternal kingdom. Salvation had finally come.

But our salvation cannot be guaranteed unless we made a committed choice to give everything to God through faith, hope and love. By doing so, we will become a part of God though we are still in this valley of tears. We cannot ascend to the new heavens unless we become an integral part of God's Body but fully integrated to the God-man Christ Jesus the path to eternal happiness can become reality. But it takes the death of our own corruptible body that perfect integration be possible and with the help of all His members His church benefited everyone.

It was only our Lady who clearly understood why the one true God must become three persons so to accomplished His masterpiece. Like her intimate union with the Three Persona, our Lady is also united to the three mystical Body of Christ. (Church).

The three Persona of the Church as follows:

1. The Church Militant are the active living members who were baptized and confirmed by the Catholic Church. Baptism enrolled them as real integral parts of God's Body and the baptized had the greatest responsibility in fully following the Head which is Christ. He gave us Sacred Scriptures as His perfect manual of instructions so our knowledge will grow into love and into His servitude. He appointed and anointed a visible church to represent Him so it will guide us to the way, the truth and the life. When He ascended to heaven Jesus fulfilled His promised to remain with His Body by giving us His Third Persona, the Holy Spirit. The same Holy Spirit who formed the Second Persona will be with us till the end of time for His function was to complete into perfection the uncompleted works of the Father and the Son. Without the Holy Spirit, God's work will be incomplete or imperfect. But God is perfection and it was His masterful design to make Himself available in Three Persons to make His greatest works brought to reality. In transforming us into God involved the greatest effort and time for the degree of difficulty immeasurable and only God can make it possible but He needs help from the other Two Persona.

In Sacred Scriptures, we can conclude the great difficulties of God guiding creation in doing His holy will. It was and is a love and hate relationship between the two diverse being that union between God and man is not possible. God being Him never give up on us knowing that His masterpiece if completed brings Him the greatest glory and joy. God will remain always with us since the beginning and He was always guiding His chosen people drawing them showing the awesome power enticing them to stick with Him by making promises. At that time, their pilgrimage to the new earth and the new heaven was still so far and remote and to console them God made a covenant. He promised them that they will have the promised land filled with milk and honey. Since His people were deprived of freedom and material blessings they looked forward for God's promised land where they will have their freedom and abundant corporal blessings. Creation after its eviction from the Garden of Eden were so deprived of material and spiritual blessings but God made a covenant with Noah, Abraham, Isaac, Jacob and Moses promising them an adequate replacement of paradise lost. By doing so, God was enticing and drawing them hoping they will stick with Him and get closer than before.

But despite God's goodness His chosen people kept on running away from Him by rebelling and when punished they called and cried out to Him and always God delivered them from His judgement. They can never have peace with their God no matter how they tried to obey His commandments for the simple reason that the Prince of Peace had not yet come. We who are now the militant church received God's greatest spiritual blessings with the Presence of His Second Persona who brought peace to the world by reconciling us to God the Father.

And more blest we are spiritually for the Third Persona will remain with us till the end of time ensuring that the works of the Father and the Son will not be in vain. He had renewed the phase of the earth and the Holy Spirit will be the One who will restore the beauty of our soul. He will not stop inspiring us to do God's will and to draw us to the Body of Christ so we can receive those powerful potent sacraments of the Catholic Church. One had to be a mystical theologian to see how powerful those sacraments that God equipped His Body with all kinds of weapons and ammunition that Satan and his legions trembled with fear. Unlike the old covenant where Jesus had not yet come, we are indeed more blest than them because of the Holy Spirit and the Catholic Church.

The Holy Spirit is the perfect guide of Holy Mother Church where God constantly inspires and directs the universal leader to act and move in accordance to His will. The Papacy was installed to govern and lead God's flock knowing that the narrow way is so difficult to enter. Even our Lord hinted that it is much easier for a camel to enter the eye of the needle than the worldly to enter His kingdom. We can only enter the narrow way by our abject poverty of spirit and it is the Holy Spirit who inspires us to enter into intimacy with the Holy Trinity.

The Church Militant's journey to their eternal home is much much more demanding than the journey to the promised land. It is so difficult because the transforming process takes so much of God and of course more so of us. And without the hard persistent works of the Third Persona it would be impossible to turn dust into divinity. For the

Holy Spirit will give us His gifts of wisdom, knowledge, understanding, counsel, fortitude, piety and the fear of the Lord. When one receives those gifts from the Holy Spirit one becomes the dwelling place of God. And the one who received His gifts have the greatest responsibility not to grieve the heavenly Guest by committing sin. The person who perseveres in living the life of the Spirit will continue to possessed that precious gifts leading it to holiness and perfection and will bear the fruits of God. These fruits of God are charity, joy, peace, patience, kindness, goodness, generosity, faithfulness, modesty, humility, gentleness, self control and chastity. Once the person have the fruits of God the process of its transformation had speed up to the highest level and it is now united with the Triune God. Such tremendous works was done by the Holy Spirit and it was Jesus who fulfilled His promise to us that He will sent the Paraclete. It is the same Holy Spirit who entered into our Lady's womb and the holy Infant God was her fruit. The same divine principle will apply to us if He remains in us. Perfection and holiness can only be accomplished with the indwelling of the Holy Spirit but our greatest challenge is to make sure He stayed permanently. Paul shared his experiences about holiness and perfection.

"Not as though I had already attained, either were already perfect; but I follow after, if that I may apprehend. For that which also I am apprehended of Christ Jesus." (Philippians 3:12).

Like Paul called to the highest life of God, we too must embrace His calling even the journey will be most difficult and most demanding because the Triune God will always be with us making sure we make it. With our Savior seated at the right hand of the Eternal Father unceasingly praying for His Body left on earth, with our Holy Mother Church and its powerful potent sacraments, with our Lady's powerful help and intercession and finally with the Presence of God, the Third Persona's intense involvement for our transformation should give us the greatest hope and the greatest confidence that we will make it. But the enemies of our salvation specially Satan will keep deceiving and lying to hide from us the fullness of God's truth. To listen to him keep us from believing of what the Catholic Church had done for all.

As pilgrims, it is so challenging to walk the narrow path and no doubt we will slip and fall every day but we should never get discouraged nor dismayed with our faults and failures since this was a part of the cross we have to embrace and carry and we need each other to encourage and to inspire so we gain His strength to power us into God's waiting arms. Our Lady encourages us never never give up but to persevere in God's love doing His way to the end. For at the finish line salvation will be ours if and only we cling to God.

"Praying always with all prayer and supplication in the Spirit and watching there unto with all perseverance and supplications for all saints." (Ephesians 6:1).

It is our Lady's powerful prayers that the church continuously called on her holy name.

"Hail Mary full of grace."

"Holy Mary, mother of God pray for us sinners now and at the hour of our death. Amen."

If one can only see how many souls were saved by our Lady's pleading, the whole world will call upon her name and every person will be carrying the Rosary beads for truly the mother of God was and is the most hardest and persistent worker in our Lord's vineyard. Our Lady received the greatest gift and Mary knew she had the greatest responsibility in helping us reaching our heavenly home.

She is the captain of the new Noah's ark (The Catholic Church) and she guides and navigates her children away from the perilous path of the vast unpredictable ocean. The seas are deceitful, tranquil and peaceful at first then suddenly strong winds and vicious waves that can capsized the ship but in her hands is God's power and might and always our Lady keep us safe. Anytime and whatever Mary asked from Him, God will never refused His beloved, knowing that His obedient daughter never refused anything He asked of her. Whatever is the peril or risk or danger we will encounter one is truly safe and secure as long as we cling to our mother.

"Mother behold thy son."

Our Savior reminded her never lose sight of us. And she never did and never will.

This is the reason why the Catholic Church in every place and corner of the world had a statue or a portrait of the Blessed Virgin Mary as a lasting tribute and to honor her in doing God's work. And doing it for us. This is the reason why our Lady appeared to Dominic to pray and promote the prayer of the Holy Rosary so many souls will be save through her powerful and persistent intercession. It was St. Dominic who founded the great religious order, the Order of Preachers who defended the church against great heresies inspired by her enemies. And her chosen son, Dominic did by the constant prayer of the Holy Rosary and his religious order spread all over the world and produced many distinguished saints who imitated and followed their great founder.

It was God's mother whom Dominic revered and loved that made him famous and it was her intercession that Dominic in 1221 fiercely fought and preached against the great heresy of the Albigensian. They have published their brilliant writing about the many errors and faults of the Catholic Church but the greatest heresy was that according to them that Christ is not human. Such heresy threatened the Catholic Church during the 12th and 13th centuries and since many believed them with their own brilliant writings, Dominic did not stop preaching and he never stop defending his church and the truth and honor of his Lord and God that Christ Jesus was both God and man.

Threatened by Dominic's own brilliant preaching some of the Albigensian heretics approached him and proposed a challenge. This was proposed that each side wrote an apology and three judges who were favorable of the Albigensian view were selected but when it is time to announce the decision the judges refused to proclaim the winner. The heretics wanted a different kind of trial by the use of fire reminiscent of Elijah's challenge to the prophets of Baal. They commended both books to God and the wrong book be consumed by fire.

Blessed Jordan of Saxoohy who witnessed the event saw that the Albigensian books were rapidly consumed into ashes but the book by Dominic remained intact. Amazed and not convinced they threw it to the fire a second time and third time. Such historic event strengthened the church and converted many. But it was our Lady's installation of the Holy Rosary through Dominic that so many souls were converted and saved by it.

Through the prayers of the Holy Rosary, infinite blessings were given sustaining our existence. Our Lady had and has devoted and dedicated herself to all specially those who called on her protecting and saving them from all evils that surrounds us.

With Holy Mother Church and her members along with her powerful mother, our pilgrimage will be much safer and secure if we remain faithful, dedicated and devoted to our Lord, our Lady and to the one and only true church, the Catholic Church.

REFLECTION

"And I say also unto thee, that thou art Peter, and upon this rock I will build my church; and the gates of hell shall not prevail against it." (Matthew 16:18).

God's will was to establish only one Church to shepherd His flock. Thus, the great commission was given to Peter who became the first to head the Papacy. The Pope is the Vicar of Christ and the chair of Peter represents the throne of Christ the King. Christ is the Rock and Peter will represent Him once Christ ascended to His Father in heaven. Once Jesus accomplished His mission in redeeming us he also instituted His Church and the Blessed Sacrament to fulfill His promise to remain with us till the end of time. The reason why the church is invincible and indestructible is nothing more that Jesus the Rock of salvation is always present to protect and defend His Bride from all the assaults of its enemies. And so many are the enemies of the Catholic Church. Since He had ascended to the Father He accomplished two things that made our redemption and salvation possible. First, once He was back to the Father enthrone on His right was and is our eternal Priest constantly pleading for His Body still in exile but being processed. We who belongs and baptized by the Catholic Church not only benefited greatly by our Lord's powerful intercession in heaven but also greatly benefited by our own integration to His Body here on earth. In the Catholic Church God instituted the seven powerful and potent sacraments that greatly assisted, nourished and strengthened its members so it will have that abundant energy and power to persevere and not to quit the race to the new heavens. A great book, YBA A CATHOLIC reveals why the Catholic Church is the only one true church that taught the fullness of truth. In this book one will know and understand what it means to be a Catholic and also one's responsibility to truly live as one. Of course, to attract attention and to gather as much followers it can deceived so many called religious leaders established their very own church also claiming and lying that they are the real deal. Unfortunately so many fell into such trappings thereby risking their immortal souls into eternal damnation. Again, let it be known that the Chair of Peter in Rome is the head of the one and only true church established by Christ Himself not man.

Disagreements and arguments will never end but only one church was appointed and anointed by God and the others were merely establish by the will of man and not God.

PRAYER

Holy Mary, mother of our Savior, pray for us Body of your Divine Son struggling against all the enemies of our salvation and do obtain for us poor sinners but members of His Body all the graces necessary for our safe and secure journey to our heavenly homeland. Our Lady of Unity, do not permit those our brothers and sisters who are led astray by false shepherds and bring them back to where they rightly belong in the bosom of the true and only church established by your beloved Son. Amen.

CHAPTER THIRTEEN
· ·
WITH HER CHURCH SUFFERING

As the Third Person of God, the Holy Spirit's function was to guide the Church Militant, while the Second Person of the Blessed Trinity's function was to incorporate the Church Suffering to His own suffering and death to perpetuate the justification of all the sins committed in the past, present and future. Theologians have concluded that our Lord's death on the cross was enough for our justification and there is no more need to pay the penalty of our sin. True, but there is also a great need that members of His Body have to make some contribution for the well being of the church. There is that great need that the Church Militant must offer themselves as a living sacrifice holy and acceptable to God. But the sufferings and sacrifices of the Church Militant merely scratch the surface in contributing for the expiation of our sins. Although Christ did paid the penalty for our sins past, present and future, our affinity for sin had not changed at all. This is the reason why the history of our existence never changed in terms of humanity's history of pains, troubles, sickness, diseases, calamities, pestilences, famine despite all the progress we have made. All the punishment we have received since our eviction from Eden is never enough for we never stop sinning thus we have to make up that accountability for the sake of God's justice. We must continue to pay the penalty for our sins.

"And Cain said unto the Lord, my punishment is greater than I can bear." (Genesis 4:13).

Prisoners serving life sentences echoed Cain's complain. The crime of murder warrants life long sentences and even death reminding us how greatly God is offended when someone took a life that belongs to God.

Each day many lives were taken by committing such evil act. Many suffered when a life is taken away unjustly. But God allowed it so we will have the opportunity in contributing our pains and miseries for the good of His Body.

"We now rejoice in my sufferings for you and fill up that which is behind of the afflictions of Christ in my flesh for his body's sake, which is the church." (Colossians 1:24).

Our Lady herself requested the three little innocent children at Fatima to offer themselves a life of prayer, penance for the conversion of sinners. As little lambs they made contribution to the Body of Christ. Two of the little children even gave up their own lives for the sake of others.

As a true member of Christ Body, anyone who offered all its sufferings or afflictions for the conversion of sinners and for the salvation of souls will gain great graces for its very own salvation. Even the simplest form of labor if offered heartily will gain merits in God's eyes.

"In the sweat of thy face shalt thou eat bread, till thou return unto the ground." (Genesis 3:19).

Despite all the advance technology in growing fruits and vegetables, there remains in our world the continuous suffering of hunger and thirst. Missionaries who spent time serving the poorest of the poor worked feverishly in providing for them by soliciting funds from the wealthy but still it does not suffice. Still, widows and orphans searched garbage bins for their meals and others eating mud pies and drinking polluted water despite all the great efforts of the church and charitable organization, the poor and destitute remains. More sufferings are needed for the good of the church.

We must continue to suffer and all the sick, aged, mentally ill and in firmed have no choice but to bear its afflictions again echoing the agony of Cain.

"My punishment is greater than I can bear".

Our Lady knew all our miseries but she reminds us that we can make great use of them by turning the curses of sin into the greatest blessings. She reminded us how the greatest curse of witnessing her Son crucified cruelly on the cross turned into the greatest blessings mankind will ever receive. Who can compare such blessing when the new heavens are now open and available to us. This is the greatest fruit of the cross and we are invited to carry it patiently and embracing it as our immortal treasure. Refusing to carry and embrace our cross is nothing else but the rejection of God's greatest gift - our salvation. Most of us will find so much difficulties when confronted with afflictions and infirmities for our bodies are governed by the flesh and will never accept nor embrace whatever is not pleasant, comfortable or desirable. Our flesh wants to have all the comfort, ease, leisure and any discomfort or disagreeable to the five senses, it will rebel. Thus to accept and embrace anything that is disagreeable will be a battle. These are the primary reason why most if not all of us cannot take or embrace or even tolerate what is not pleasant to our bodies. This is why we marginalized suffering's true and real value. Our preference in avoiding the cross does diminishes our desire for God. We do desire Him but in the context of our feelings and emotion and nothing more. Only those who are deeply spiritual understood that if we let our flesh governs us we are considered God's enemies.

"Because the carnal mind is enmity against God: for it is not subject to the law of God, neither indeed can be. So then they that are in the flesh cannot please God." (Romans 8:7-8)

This warning was constantly repeated again and again by our Lady in all her appearances reminding us to repent to do penance and to pray always so we can conquer our greatest enemy - our very own flesh.

"For if ye live after the flesh, ye shall die; but if ye through the Spirit do mortify the deeds of the body, ye shall live." ((Romans 8:12)

This is our greatest problem - us. Freewill is God's great gift to us since we can chose freely our own future and most importantly our eternity. If we chose to conform our will to God then we have the greatest chance to spent eternity in the new heavens but if we chose not to then we are already dead spiritually.

God sent His greatest apostle Paul to preached and write for our greatest benefits so we can get to heaven. Paul received from our Lord His instructions for our conversion, sanctification and salvation and that can only be done by living in God's Spirit and nothing else. Those who passionately live in the flesh definitely belongs to the devil and those who passionately live in God's Spirit belongs to God. Simple thoughts to remember but loaded with wisdom since the Holy Spirit's function was to make perfect and complete the works of the Father and the Son.

"For as many as are led by the Spirit of God, they are the sons of God." (Romans 8:14)

It is the Third Person of the Holy Trinity that will make us sons and daughters of God. As our Lady was espoused to the Holy Spirit so are those whose lives are filled with Him. This is the same Spirit that formed

Christ in Mary's womb. The same Spirit who will transform those who follow and live the gospel preached and taught by the Second Persona of God. Those living in the flesh cannot be transformed because Spirit is its greatest enemy and its instinct was for its own survival and own passion for gratification and it will fight and rebel against the Spirit. Simply, for the sake of our immortal soul to live in God's Spirit we are united with the Triune God giving us the greatest chance to possessed God forever.

"And if children then heirs; heirs of God, and joint heirs with Christ; if be so that we suffer with him, that we may be also glorified together." (Romans 8:17).

Indeed, as the glorious apostle of Christ, Paul reminded us, if so be we suffer with him.

There is no other creature that suffered so much than our Lady and for her sufferings she was greatly glorified by the Father, Son and Holy Spirit. Those who truly desired to become true and real children of God and co heirs with Christ must also accept and embrace with gratitude whatever sufferings sent to our lives. To reject them, will be our great loss.

As our Lady continues her mission appearing to the ends of the earth always asking her children to do penance and to offer their sufferings so soul can be save. Several of her apparition showed tears of blood from her eyes of our Lady's statue. Such phenomena cannot be explained but it cannot be also ignored or denied because there was a message behind the unusual event.

It was revealed to the community that our Lady's eyes saw from the cross at Calvary the blood of God pouring down into the earth until nothing remains. She reminded us those blood were for us and not to take for granted nor marginalized her Son's sacrifices so all can enter the new heavens.

She also emphasized the great importance offering all our pains and sufferings uniting it to her Son's suffering for it will bring abundant graces to creation. The Catholic Church of which His Son as the head had been greatly divided and broken by its unfaithful and sinful members wounding severely the Body of Christ and everyone is called to help heal its wound. By accepting and offering our sufferings will bring healing and cure to His Body constantly contaminated by the sinfulness, infidelities and gross imperfections of its members. Without the offerings and sacrifices of the faithful and devout members of His Body it would die and such death will bring the end of times and all will finally see the terrifying judgement that no eyes want to see. However, the Body of Christ will never die despite the incurable infestation of sins brought by unfaithful and neglectful members for God as its Head will not die. And with the intense involvement of the Holy Spirit members will be inspired to become a willing sacrificial victim for the sake of the Church.

"He was oppressed and he was afflicted yet he opened not his mouth; he is brought as a lamb to the slaughter, and as a sheep before her shearers is dumb, so he opened not his mouth." (Isaiah 53:7).

Indeed, the gates of hell will not prevail against His church for in His Body are many members who followed their Master courageously carried their crosses denying themselves of anything that displeases their Head. Such faithful followers in His church will bring powerful healing to His wounded Body.

"But he was wounded for our transgression, he was bruised for our iniquities; the chastisement of our peace is upon him; and with his stripes we are healed." (Isaiah 53:5).

But despite of those faithful followers, our Lady informed us that it is never enough to counter act the sins committed every moment of the day. Besides, there are not many truly faithful followers of the Lamb who can truly imitate Him as active participants of God's saving works. Our Lady knew the whole world would be destroyed and brought to judgement unless another way or means that can help in satisfying God's perfect justice. With the fullness of God's grace and with her fervent prayers, conceived and came into existence the second mystical Body of Christ who will greatly satisfies God's justice.

The Church Suffering or Purgatory where billions of souls are members united with the sufferings of the Church Militant made possible the sustenance of the life of the world. Those who suffered in this prison of purgation does appease God's divine justice which our sufferings could not. In Purgatory, the sufferings and pains of one soul is much more than what the whole world suffered. It is the Church Suffering in union with the Church Militant and the Church Triumphant are the truly acceptable and even pleasing to God for such unity made the church of God truly invincible and indestructible as prophesied by God Himself. Though only one church its composition is three which corresponded to the Three Persona of God so our perfection and holiness would be made possible and attainable. With the monotheistic God, it is not possible. But with the Triune God everything can now work to perfection.

The same principle applies to His church. She needed her other two bodies so we can reach our heavenly destination. It was our Lady's revelation to her community that the souls in purgatory had the most powerful influence on God since their intense sufferings are comparable to hell and the only difference is that the soul in hell will never have the chance of getting out while the soul in purgatory are guaranteed that sooner or later they will be admitted in heaven and will be with their God. In fact, the souls in purgatory rejoices unceasingly for they won salvation and even joyful of their pains of purgation knowing that soon very soon they will received the rewards promised to them. It is the Church Suffering or the souls in purgatory that God's extreme punishment of all sins had been satisfied for what they suffered was almost what Christ suffered on the cross. Indeed, purgatory is God's greatest invention but disregarded by skeptics and heretics because of their deprivation of the fullness of truth. The Church Suffering was our Lady's pleading to her Father to her Son and to her Spouse in establishing Purgatory for the sake of saving many more souls that otherwise would have been claimed by Satan as his. Had Purgatory not existed only a handful few will be save. With it, God will be greatly glorified and greatly honored and praised for the great numbers of multitudes will be rejoicing and praising Him for all eternity. If the heavens rejoices with one single soul saved what more if there are millions or even billions. Thus, Purgatory added more honor and glory to Him that made it.

REFLECTION

"Without not correction from the child; for if thou beat him with the rod, he shall not die. Thou shall beat him a rod, and shall deliver his soul from hell". (Proverbs 23:13-14).

Baptized them in the name of the Father the Son and the Holy Spirit. This was the last command to His apostles when Jesus ascended to heaven. With baptism one became the child of God. And when one becomes God's child He will correct and admonish it like a real living father who wants your greatest and highest good. To whom God loves He punishes. But because of our strong stubborn will, God had became our adversary and He imposed severe punishment if we continue to fight against His will. We struggled with such issue because what God's want of us constantly contradicts our own desire and the love we have in the world also added to this pressing problem. Yes, indeed we love free will for we simply do what pleases us. But the One who made us had different plans and to make sure we are in the same page with God He like a real loving father will exercise His own will to correct and punish us with His rod. This rod can come in any shape, form or event such an incurable disease, illness, financial ruins, divorce, broken relationship, troubled life, tragedies, spiritual dryness or blindness and every kind of pains and afflictions imaginable. God knows that if He neglect to use His rod and never intervene certainly eternal death follows. But with this continuous beating of God's rod will bring us to our senses forces us to redirect our undisciplined will allowing Him to direct us to His.

Our beatings from His rod forces us to listen and think what God was trying to do with us. Finally, with His enlightenment we realized that what we had suffered from the beatings will indeed deliver us from the fires of hell. Despite all the beatings and lashes we received in this life will never be enough to make up for all the sins we committed and after death there still remains some debt to be paid.

Thus, Purgatory was God's greatest invention as the final phase of our beatings so no stain or a speck of sin remains. We all knew that even the most holy in us does fall at least seven times a day what more the majority of us swimming in sin. Although we did received our beatings here on earth it does not completely remove all the stain, all the filth and all impurities and this is the greatest logical reason that Purgatory was so essential and so necessary to make us perfectly cleansed and purified making us so ready to face our God. The Catholic Church were wrongly accused that Purgatory was its own invention but the truth is no man could ever come up with such brilliant idea for our highest and greatest good but God.

PRAYER

Hail holy mother of God, mother of sorrows, pray for us exiled children of God by obtaining for us the grace of holy final perseverance. As you have dealt with all kinds of sorrows and affliction keep us always in your maternal care and protection and pray for us to obtain the virtue of patience, endurance and strength to keep on going to our heavenly destination. Stay beside on your helpless and vulnerable children weakened and discouraged by our sinfulness and blindness and obtain for us His graces that we may join all the saints in heaven there to praise and worship the Blessed Trinity and to thank you for being our mother. Amen

CHAPTER FOURTEEN

· ·

WITH HER TRIUMPHANT CHILDREN

"There are they which were not defiled with women; for they are virgins. These are they which follow the Lamb wither ever he goeth. These were redeemed from among men being the first fruits unto God and to the Lamb." (Revelation 14:4).

Our great Lady who bore the blessed fruit in her womb changed everything that the Hand of God made. We were formed with His Hands but the result seemed disastrous for Adam and Eve failed in obeying God's command. Obviously there was an absence of love in the Garden of Eden. Had both possessed the love that Jesus had for His Father, Adam would never have disobeyed God. Or both possessed the love of our Lady to her God neither would have been evicted and punished severely. It was the absence of pure perfect love that provoke God's anger towards His own handiwork.

"And the Lord said. I will destroy man whom I created from the face of the earth; both man, and beast, and the creeping thing, and the fowls of the air; for it repenteth and that I have made them." (Genesis 6:7).

Since God is all love He was filled with sorrow and regret knowing that the works of His Hands failed to live in His love. God's purpose in creating us was that we will learn how to love but how could they learn when the teacher and master of love had not come into the world depriving them His teaching and example. Yet, we wonder why God did not execute His judgement when obviously they deserve death. Why did not God wipe out everything?

"But Noah found grace in the eyes of the Lord." (Genesis 6:8).

Our Lady keep reminding us that every day thousands and thousands of souls were lost because of our gross negligence and disregard of His greatest grace, our salvation. As in the old days where God was rejected by His creation, the same attitude remains as we keep choosing to do our own will. When we chose to do our own will, the result were always disastrous and it reinforces what our Lady warns.

But despite our stiff necked attitude, our Lady never lose hope and she never gives up laboring harder with her constant apparition reminding us not to lose our immortal soul to things that are base and worthless. Even though our Lady is filled with sorrow she found consolation and joy that millions and millions of souls that would have been lost were saved by the existence of Purgatory. And every time she appeared to them during her feast days, purgatory is transformed heaven-like where the pains and sufferings temporarily stop and they were filled with joy before her presence. All her suffering children were greatly consoled every time she visited them surrounded by the multitude of angelic host and such glorious scenery filled them with joyous ecstasy thanking and praising God that they were spared and were saved by the existence of Purgatory. It was the intercessory prayers of the Church Militant and the Church Triumphant that gives the souls in Purgatory a brief taste of their heavenly home. Every Holy Mass offered to them brings the souls in Purgatory the greatest relief and joy knowing that they are forever save and certain to be admitted in the new heavens. Once they are allowed to be admitted, our Lady of the Angels will escort them to be presented before the throne of God making them citizens and heirs of His kingdom. In God's presence they have been purified, sanctified and glorified and they have been perfectly transformed into His likeness.

"And in their mouth was found no guile; for they are without fault before the throne of God." (Revelation 14:5).

There is no one who is free from the stain of sin that even the most holy and righteous will at least fell seven times a day and all has to be paid for the satisfaction of God's justice. What more the negligent and the godless who never thought about their eternal welfare. What more of the unbelievers who simply rejected God? What more those who were deceived by false religion and pastors who taught the wrong way. What more those who simply are too busy and too engross with their own and worldly endeavor? No wonder that thousands and thousands of souls were lost each day and by God's mercy and kindness thousands were given reprieved because of the powerful intercession of the Church Militant. So many thousands also were saved from hell because of the intercession of the Church Triumphant and were instead brought to Purgatory. Without the church established by our Lord and God, only a handful will be save. But with the three mystical church, the world is not completely lost and yes, we are so blest and privilege because the true church established by Christ had done marvelous things in saving millions of souls. But the world had no clue that it was our Lady's marvelous ministry that resulted in an abundant harvest of souls.

"And Jesus said unto him, verily I say unto thee, to day shalt thou be with me in paradise." (Luke 23:43).

Saved souls became an integral part of the Church Triumphant. They have triumphed because they did God's will. The Church Triumphant begin its formation at the foot of the cross as our Lord was ready to expire, the opening of the new heavens was also closing in to admit all who were listed in the Book of Life will now be rewarded according to His promise. And it was the most despicable and repulsive sinner a common criminal receiving the greatest privilege to enter heaven and to be with his Savior who fulfilled the promise while still on the cross.

"Remember me when you get into your kingdom, Jesus,"

It was a powerful acknowledgement that Jesus alone can save and bring us to heaven. But nobody knew that while the hoopla was on the crucifixion drama that it was our Lady's powerful prayer interceding for the two hopeless criminals knowing they were certainly bound for hell. These two who were crucified with Jesus on Calvary grace was obtained by our Lady and they have the greatest opportunity to avoid eternal death. The good thief chose wisely by humbling himself before God confessing that Jesus is God and King and salvation was his while the other one remain obstinate and his judgement only known by Him. The dramatic salvation scene was recorded so the whole world and the coming generations will know that only through Jesus Christ that salvation is possible. But also hidden was our powerful great Lady's intercession that brought those saving grace of which she had in full. Our Lady never wasted the gifts she received from God by applying all His graces entrusted to her exemplified by the conversion of the good thief on Calvary. Once Jesus gave up His last breathe the new heavens opened and the Church Triumphant was established and one notable member was the most unworthy member but deserving simply because of our lady who is mother of salvation and mother of the church.

"It is finished." (John 19:30).

Once Jesus gave up His very Life, the Church Triumphant became even more powerful with the mass exodus where hundreds of thousand listed on the Book of Life were integrated. All the prophets, patriarchs and all of God's servants of the old covenant did finally received their long awaited reward. As soon as our Lord gave up His Life the old earth was destroyed reconstructed as the new earth begins its reign. Christ the King had come to establish His invincible and indestructible church so it can destroy all the enemies of God. He invented that His church will have three powerful functions much like His very Own Three powerful Persona.

As the monotheistic God cannot complete His masterpiece without the other Persona so does Holy Mother Church must have its three powerful bodies otherwise we can never enter the new heaven. The first body, the Militant Church and its members cannot be united with the Church Triumphant without first entering itself into the realms of the Church Suffering. Such design was not man's imagination but rather invented by the supreme Mind of God. Our good and great God did everything possible so we can be save. If we do not appreciate nor value or treasured Him then truly we deserved to be with Satan in hell. But our Lady does not want anyone of her children to be lost. She wants everyone to join the Church Militant in our journey to the victorious Church Triumphant, of course after stopping by and passing through the Church Suffering. Our Lady emphasized the greatest importance to become a Catholic. God gave us such awesome and marvelous means so we can truly make it. She warned that if we chose and embrace other religion the risk of losing our soul increases exponentially. There is no other greater security and safety when one is baptized and confirmed in the Catholic Church since one's integration to the real Body of Christ greatly benefited the member because in it were housed a treasury of graces unavailable in any churches or in any religion.

Our Lady's powerful participation in the Catholic Church have brought and delivered so many distinguished and honored saints that are now integrated to His Church Triumphant increasing its invincibility and indestructibility where their reward was oneness with the Triune God. As the Holy Spirit dwells, guides and inspires the Church Militant, the Church Suffering united its purifying punishment to our Lord Jesus' suffering and death on the cross while our Father in heaven awaits those triumphant souls to crown them. The First Persona is indeed the Alpha and the Omega where in the beginning He pick up a worthless dust molded it in His image destroying it recreating it and in the end God receives us to be His very own.

If we do not join the true church, we will be deprived of knowing our Lady's triumphant children who truly earned their glorious crown through the fullness of her teachings, through the marvelous and mystical works of the three churches and through the most powerful intercession of our great and most honored Lady. These are only a few of her triumphant children who made great impact in the Catholic Church bringing more souls to God.

It was Francis of Assisi whom our Lady admired for his full love of God by imitating Jesus' life of poverty and extreme penances so he can participate with the church's mission in bringing more souls to God. Francis truly lived the life of Christ to perfection that our Lord gifted him the stigmata where he received the wounds of Christ in Francis' hands, feet and side. He was chosen to shed his own blood in union with the blood of Christ shed in Calvary for the salvation of many souls. God chose him because Francis chose Him to be his All. And our Lady gave Francis the greatest compliment.

"Of all the triumphant souls no one closely resembled her Son than Francis".

Such compliment can be manifested by how Francis and his religious order became so powerful that spread all over the world inspiring and drawing even more souls for God. If you are not a member of the true church you will never know how this triumphant son had accomplished and achieved his victory against all odds. And the Franciscan Order have produced and delivered many great and powerful saints through their founder's intercession.

An important thought to be remembered was about the great Hindu, Mahatma Ghandi's desire to become a Christian after throughly reading and studying the Bible but after observing and noticing Christian missionaries and charismatic preachers he changed his mind and when asked he replied that what they were teaching and preaching about Christ themselves were not doing.

It was well documented that Mahatma Ghandi's life also resemble Francis life by the way they lived, loved, served and sacrificed for the greater good of others and he after reading and studying sacred scriptures applied it in his life. Had Ghandi met Francis they would have been a powerful force.

Another triumphant son of the church was the great St. Dominic whom our Lady choose to spread devotion to the Holy Rosary and the whole world have no clue how this prayer promoted by our Lady have positively effected us. It was the prayer that defeated the Albigensian heresy which threatened to destroy the church but once our Lady intervened it was quickly suppressed. And once Dominic joined the Church Triumphant, his powerful intercessions for his religious Order produced many more outstanding saints such as St. Thomas Aquinas, St. Catherine of Siena, St. Rose of Lima and a long list of other known saints belonging to the Dominican Order. If you do not belong to the Catholic Church, you have cheated yourself greatly of its treasures and divine benefits.

Then, there is Mother Teresa of Calcutta, Pope John Paul the great who had drawn many back to the church and recently Pope Francis I. It takes many volumes and books to list the blessed names of triumphant souls that the Catholic Church had produced as a shining example to the world that truly this was and is the real and true church. There are hundreds of thousands Catholic saints that have done great and outstanding works for the Triune God and most importantly was how they lived their lives in imitation of Christ. If you are privilege to go the Vatican library in Rome the lives of this triumphant souls were recorded and documented in the treasury of the church. The Catholic Church had many millions or even billions of enemies for she is the only true and only church that bring true salvation to the world. Satan is vent and furious in destroying what Christ build through Peter knowing this church took away millions of souls belonging to him. She will carry and unite us to her other body, the Church Triumphant where we are welcome and finally crowned by the Triune God. The Catholic Church is not merely a church denomination or institution but truly the real Body of Christ.

And it is always our Lady's hope that all should come and be a part of it.

REFLECTION

"He that find his life shall lose it: And he that lose his life for my sake shall find it." (Matthew 10:39).

Once again a painful reminder that in order to reach our heavenly home takes more than what others taught is easy by simply accepting and acknowledging that Jesus is Lord and Savior. However the cliche, no pain no gain comes into play and indeed very much applicable to our journey and the possession of eternal life and happiness promised by God to us. Why it is so? Why it is not that easy to be save? Have you tried to lose fifty pounds of weigh when you are so addicted with food? Waking up early in the cold mornings for an hour of exercise and once done hunger takes over but because of our determination to exercise and diet we suffer from fatigue and the pangs of an angry stomach. The smell of fresh coffee entices our senses and the desire to have something sweet for our morning meal. At noon, we heard our stomach growling demanding food but we must stick to our strict discipline and constant control otherwise we will never lose that ugly fat that weighed us down. If losing fifty pounds of fat involves a lot of sacrifices, denial, discipline and pain for the good and health for our body what more is when our immortal soul is involved? Those who were deceived by false teachers and shepherds that it is easy to be saved are so many and the truth is, they are not.

Salvation involves the complete transformation of self into the highest form of life which we can never obtain unless aided by the Triune God through the marvelous ministry of His church. Precious words by our Teacher that we all should do so we can truly be transformed was simply, to lose our life so we can His life. To lose one's life is nothing else but complete detachment from the lesser things and to gain God's Life is simply to live the life of Jesus through His teaching and always abiding to His will.

As member of His Body one has to deny itself by carrying our crosses and such sacred activities indeed passed His criteria of losing one's life for His sake.

PRAYER

Hail holy queen, enthrone in heaven look with pity on your pilgrim church struggling in our difficult and demanding journey to the highest life. Obtain for us our Lady of Grace that God will grant us the commitment and conviction to detach ourselves from the things that enslaves us and to strive for the highest life that He had plans for us. Our Lady of Wisdom, obtain for us the grace to persevere and not be dismayed by our weaknesses and failures knowing that perseverance will get us through. O holy Mary, mother of the Church let us never be separated from His Body and let its sacraments be that transforming agent that will gain us Your Son's Life. Amen.

CHAPTER FIFTEEN
WITH HER MISSION

In the history of God and man many distinguished themselves by how they served and honored God. We heard Noah's righteousness and his obedience to God by building the ark preserving creation from annihilation from His wrath. He also obeyed God by gathering animals in pairs so it will replenish the multitude that was lost during the flood. Noah's obedience and righteousness made him great.

Abraham also was great for his blind obedience to God when he was asked to sacrifice his only beloved son, Isaac and by doing so, God rewarded him making Abraham father of many nations. From Abraham's son Isaac came the twelve tribe of Israel chosen to be God's people.

Then came Moses, the great prophet who was chosen to lead and free Israel from the bondage of slavery. Moses was called by God to also lead His people into the Promised land. It was the Mosaic law that the way to God was introduced not only to His chosen people but eventually to the Gentiles and to the whole world. We knew the great men called and chosen by God such as David, Solomon, the prophet Isaiah, Elijah and many more who distinguished themselves in the Old Testament.

John the Baptist came and our Lord praised him as there was no other prophet greater than John. He was chosen to prepare the coming of the Messiah.

As the old covenant about to be replace by the coming of the Messiah, Jesus came with His twelve disciples who wrote the Gospel telling and teaching the world of the way, the truth and the life. Peter distinguished himself as the shepherd being chosen by Christ to be the leader of the church. As the first pope, Peter was instructed by Christ to feed His sheep through the ministry of the true church. Paul became known as the greatest apostle for his unceasing works in preaching and teaching the Gospel. Paul's magnificent writings became the model of how to live the perfect Christian life. These great men and devoted servants of God became known and famous and they will remain so until the end of time. They did accomplished their mission as God's chosen ones.

The list goes on as many distinguished themselves as servants of God and they did their mission of preaching the good news to all the ends of the earth. God in His plan was exalted and glorified by the many distinguished servants who did their job well. They earned and deserved God's reward for their fruitful labors.

Now as time closes in, it is time for all of humanity to honor and recognize the greatest servant and the greatest of all missionaries and that is our Lady of Unity. She is the Lady of Fatima, the Lady of Lourdes, the Lady of Grace, the Lady of Guadalupe, the Lady of Knock, the Lady of Medjajurde, the Lady of Akita, the Lady of Mount Carmel and the list gets longer. It is time for us to honor the greatest of our race and God's greatest laborer so the most Holy Trinity will be greatly honored and glorified. We do not offend nor sinned against the good God if we do so for without her yes humanity will be lost forever. God is glorified and honored not once but thrice if we do homage to the mother of Jesus and to embrace her as our very own mother. Had our Lady refused the Eternal Father there is no other who qualifies to take her place and God's work cannot be completed. By her yes, God immediately bestowed on her His fullness thus making God's plan in transforming us to divinity into reality. By her perfect cooperation to the holy will of God, Mary was crowned and celebrated as the Queen of heaven and earth. She deserves to be exalted and greatly honored because it was her yes that our salvation made possible. All the great prophets, patriarchs, apostles, martyrs and all the saints rejoices in the presence of their queen knowing that it was our Lady that gave them Jesus. The titles and honors she received is not enough for without her yes God's plan will not be done. We who are exile in this dark and miserable world cannot see nor think of what she had done for us and how could we when we could hardly see and understand what Jesus did for us. If we claimed we do, how is it that we remain cold and indifference to His calling and teachings. Jesus and Mary is our greatest model in perfect obedience, humility and love. Those who imitated their ways will surely win the immortal crown of God's glory. We are intimidated with Mary's holiness but if we truly examine her life she was just as ordinary and simple as us. The only difference was she never say no to God. Billions of her children does not even know that she is truly our mother for she was given to us as our greatest helper and intercessor so we can make it to heaven. Of course, it is our Lord and Savior that saves but it does not hurt nor reduce our chances but rather greatly help by having both in our side. If one is truly wise, why not have two powerful intercessors instead of one? God knew the hardships and obstacles we are facing and Mary was provided for us having all His fullness.

Our Lady is not only queen of heaven but also was enthroned queen of earth so all creation will be inspired that one of their own was placed in the highest pedestal reserved for the truly greats. There is no mystery in our Lady's greatness for she was a very simple lowly creature and she was exalted because of never refusing God. We can become like her by simply saying yes to God all the time. Indeed that is the easiest way to salvation. All the preachings and teachings about our salvation can become complicated and even burdensome but actually salvation can be easy and simple by following the path of our Lady's life or in short imitating her ways. All the teachings of our Lord that is being taught by the apostles can be easily understood and practiced by simply learning and knowing from our Lady of Unity. Isn't she the mother of our Lord? Isn't she responsible for teaching the teacher? Isn't she responsible in dispensing all the graces she received? Let us be reminded that the fullness of grace she received, Mary immediately passed on to the holy Infant Child growing in her womb. What Jesus taught and preached was the fullness of God that Mary completely gave to the One who fully gave her. Let it be known that our Lady is not after any honor or glory but simply wants to be recognize as our own mother. She only wants to help. No, our Lady had everything for she was completely one with the Triune God and all the titles and honors for her is but a dusty mist and totally worthless. When one completely possessed God, there is any more need for anything else.

But we who are exiled in this valley of tears are in most need of our Queen and mother because she is so powerful and influential with the Triune God. Again, it is worth repeating that God will never refuse her that even only with a hint God will comply. Would you not like to have her? It is truly wise to do so.

As Patroness of our salvation, our Lady was not called to preach and teach but she responded her Son's calling, mother behold thy son and she understood that He needed much help that His redeemed Body will not go astray. Also, even He is God, Jesus showed what is perfect humility by hinting He needed her help. Who do we call when in deep trouble? Of course, God. But in the business of saving our soul, Our Lady of Unity, Queen of the Church Triumphant was ordained never to stop in her ministry as his Son's greatest worker. Jesus called her knowing she is the mother of salvation and the mother of all missionaries who kept drawing others to participate in Our Lady of Unity's mission.

There is no greater missionary than our Lady of Unity. All the preachers, teachers, pastors, missionaries, apostles, prophets, theologians and all the greatest servants of God lumped together paled in comparison to our Lady's ministry in giving God all she had as His greatest ultimate helper in saving souls. Now, it is up to us to call on her help and with Jesus as Head, we can safely and surely reached our heavenly homeland.

We are reminded by Jesus the difficult path to our salvation.

"And if the righteous scarcely be saved, where shall the ungodly and the sinner appear" (1Peter 4:18).

This was Peter's warning of the truth about our salvation. He was chosen by our Lord to be the world's shepherd of soul and for that reason we have to take his message seriously. All those who preached that all you need to do is believe in our Lord Jesus Christ and salvation is ours. True but definitely deceitfully false. The truth is, it is very difficult and it takes more than believing and faith. Salvation not only involves great works but most importantly cultivating the greatness of one's love for God. Do not be deceived with those false prophets, pastors promising easy salvation without disclosing the fullness of truth. Our Lady confirms that it is so necessary for all sinners to repent and to live a righteous life and even by doing so, salvation is not guaranteed. We must get involved with our salvation by working hard for it and the assistance of God's grace. Faith by itself does not guarantee salvation. Of course, faith is necessary for it will lead to salvation. Great works and the greatest love we give Him must accompany it. We must work the hardest and tirelessly for our salvation.

"Wherefore, my beloved, as ye have always obeyed, not as in my presence only, but now much more in my absence, work out your own salvation with fear and trembling." (Philippians 2:12).

The greatest apostle and the greatest teacher of the Christian faith, Paul confirmed that there is needed a lot of hard works if one hopes to be saved. Those who preached faith alone with no works taught false and deceiving doctrines perhaps trying to entice and draw many for their own interior motives. If such is the case, one has to answer the greatness of the offense. This warning and reminder are for those whose ambition to form their own little church not equip to teach the fullness of the truth. Even if the motives was purely to lead them to our Lord the tragic fact remains that the followers are at risk losing their soul because they were deprived of so many things in regards to their salvation. Our Lady is inviting all to be baptized in the Catholic Church so one will receive all the treasures of our salvation. The Catholic Church taught that we should strive to live the highest standard of life specifically answering the calling of holiness, perfection and giving all one's love to God thus fulfilling His will. In seeking God and for the salvation of our soul, the Catholic Church encourages and inspires its flock to work very hard and diligently in obtaining it. And Holy Mother Church had proven since the beginning of its existence where thousands of her children were canonized as saints of God. The Catholic Church was and is constant and consistent in bringing home to God His lost children.

"I know thy works, that thou art lukewarm, and neither cold or hot. I will spit thee out of my mouth." (Revelation 3:15).

Clearly we should trembled with fear with His warning. He looks at our works not our belief, religion or faith but how fervent, serious and sincere we are in doing God's work. Our Lady is the hardest worker even though she had already received her glorious crown and reward for the sake of the Triune God and most importantly us.

Our Lady's mission was to make known that everyone of us should strive for perfection, holiness and to give God our greatest love. To do so, we are on the way to obtain God and heaven. Of course, to strive for the highest life of God involves tremendous work and perseverance.

"Be ye therefore perfect, even as your Father which is in heaven is perfect." (Matthew 5:48).

So many souls were lost because of their pre conceived notion that only those who were chosen can become a saint. Such thought were planted by the devil to discourage us from doing what God wants us to be. Holy and perfect. Of course we are not but we need to do it otherwise the devil had won. Our Lord's command is for our greatest and highest good and if we ignore His standard then our faith had no value. We need the element of work. It is our greatest work to become holy and perfect because we are God's greatest work. If God worked hard for us, if our Lady worked hard for us and if all God's servants worked hard for us then logically we too must become a hard or even the hardest worker for His greater glory and honor. We cannot rely on faith alone to become holy and perfect. All of the saints who won their crown in heaven were not faith slackers. How slothful and ingrate are we doing nothing when God and His faithful ones were workers extraordinaire. Examine how Paul and all Jesus apostles went to work giving everything up including life and family to build His kingdom. Even in prison deprived of bodily sustenance and comfort, Paul wrote magnificently about the things of God. Justifiably, faith alone does not make the cut. You have to show God what have you done with all the gifts and resources given to you. He had shown us how He worked hard for us. Now let us open the ledger of our life and show God which account, debit or credit had the greatest balance.

"But I say unto you, that every idle word that men shall speak, they shall give account thereof in the day of judgement." (Matthew 12:36).

Not only the idleness of your words but also your thoughts, your deeds and of course, your works. If you only show your faith, judgement cannot be done without any works. Works must be faith's constant companion.

As the world will soon closes its curtain, Our Lady of Unity's last mission was to gather all her children legitimate and illegitimate into her church under one shepherd so many many more souls will be save. She called as many responders to her religious order to become co workers in helping her Son to draw them to the church. Again and again, she told her community that tens of thousands and thousands were lost everyday because of our gross negligence, slothfulness and our stiff necked-ness. But our Lady of Unity will not be deterred in helping her Son saved as many souls as possible despite the discouraging facts. Like her Son Jesus, Mary will do everything in their powers to save souls but they have always encountered its greatest obstacle and sadly it is us. Jesus and Mary are powerless against our own will. They have been frustrated with their failures in bringing all souls to heaven because free will determines which way each of us chose.

"Because strait is the gate, and narrow is the way, which leadeth unto life, and few there be that find it." (Matthew 12:36).

Over two thousand years ago we were warned not to chose the wrong path and unfortunately like in the olden days of Noah and Sodom and Gomorrah, we remain deaf, blind invalidating God's greatest work by ignoring Him. He did everything for our greatest good. He give up His Life. He give us His mother. God gave us the Catholic Church with all its saving sacraments in helping us get through the narrow way but sad to say nothing much change in our negative attitude towards the One who truly loves us.

REFLECTION

"Hail Mary full of grace. The Lord is with you. Blessed are you among women and blessed is the fruit of your womb, Jesus. Holy Mary, mother of God pray for us sinners now and at the hour of our death. Amen."

Clearly, our Lady's mission was to dispensed all the graces she received from God. As mother of God it is also her mission to form and instruct the Child Jesus how to perfectly do the will of God, the Father. As part God, Jesus already did God's will to perfection but our Lady was doing her job perfectly in teaching the human side of her Son. As spouse of Joseph, they both shared the responsibility in taking great care of their Son. But Mary's greatest mission was to bear the fruit that will free mankind from the slavery of sin. She was to bring God to all His children. Once Jesus ascended to heaven she became the church greatest intercessor for all God's children. Once our redemption was accomplished the mother of God played the role as co redeemer helping her Son in saving sinners.

"Holy Mary, mother of God, pray for us sinners, now and at the hour of our death."

Note the church's invocation of Mary as mother of God, recognizing and acknowledging Our Lady's influencing power that can really touch the heart of the Triune God. As Jesus mission was to save all souls so does our Lady's closing mission is to save us all. But, only if we let them.

PRAYER

Our Lady of Unity, keep us your children faithful and obedient to your beloved Son's Church and obtain for us the graces that we can participate in your mission of uniting all creation under one shepherd so every one will be guided to the fullness of God's truth. As we are of different language, race, culture, custom and religion do plead to the most Holy Trinity for the graces that all will come as truly member of your Divine Son's Body, the Church. Amen.

CHAPTER SIXTEEN
. . . .
WITH HER COMMUNITY

We are a community dedicated and devoted to the most Holy Trinity, the One true God of Noah, Abraham, Isaac, Jacob and Moses in Three Divine Person fulfilling the new covenant of perfect love of God completing His works of our justification, redemption, sanctification and finally our salvation.

We were gathered by our Lady of Unity specially called to promote in honoring and glorifying the Three Persona of God so the whole world will know and understand why God must become three. The world could not fathom nor understood such mystery that even the most brilliant minds of theologians could not properly explain the complexity of the Triune God. Simply, our mind is not and cannot fathom the mind of God.

"For who hath know the mind of the Lord? Or who hath been his counselor?" (Romans 13:34).

We can never fathom such mystery that even Paul whom the Lord revealed Himself, admitted our shortcomings.

"O the depth of the riches both of the wisdom and knowledge of God! How unsearchable are his judgements, and his ways past finding out." (Romans 13:33).

Indeed, it is truly impossible to fathom the mystery of the Trinity that everybody had given up trying and to make it easier, it should remain as it was and is, a mystery. But, there is one of us, a creature who did. Yes, it is our Lady who not only fathom the Triune God but was in complete unity with each Person. For all God's creation, it is only Mary who can explain in a very simple way why each Person must enter and participate into the economy of our salvation. It is only our Lady who can properly explain why the Three Persona of God is essential and necessary for the completion of His greatest masterpiece. Our Lady intimately knew the Triune God for Mary was united with them throughout her existence. She was perfectly united to her Father, to her Son and to her Spouse, the Holy Spirit. She alone can explain why there are Three Person in God because she was the only one who entered into this mysterious concept that baffled theologians. But, to our Lady, there was no mystery at all. We, specially theologians and Bible scholars, created the mystery confusing creation into intimately knowing God even drawing us farther away from Him. The truth is, God is very simple. And our Lady, who lived the simplest life revealed to the community the simplicity of God. And she entrusted to the community the simple mission of making known to the whole world the concept of the Trinitarian God to make Him closer to us. We, the members are responsible to spread to the ends of the earth so each Person of God will be greatly honored, revered, loved and glorified. In addition, the community was entrusted that our Lady of Unity will be enshrined in all Catholic Churches. Professed members will also enshrined her in their residence together with the Bible, the book of Our Lady of Unity and The Last Testament as its own personal guide and direction in following our Lord and our Lady. Consecrated members will participate in union with our Lady in helping Jesus and His Church by inspiring and encouraging everyone to increase their knowledge of the Triune God so by knowing them increases intimacy and deeper love for God. When one is lacking in the knowledge of the Triune God, one tends to be cold and distant and its love for God stunted, worst, diminished. One cannot love without knowing. Knowing wealth can practically get us everything we desire is the reason why we are so in love with money and the prestige of being wealthy. Without knowing the value of money and wealth, one cannot simply love it or drawn to it. The same principle applies to our relationship with God. It is the lack of true knowledge why most of us are so far away from the real and living God despite His revelation, His Church and His real Presence. Thus, professed members will actively promote the great importance of truly knowing the Triune God in each Persona so many will be inspired to give God the greatest love He deserves from us.

In our Lady's community, its members are formed focusing one's spirituality may reached the highest possible state God permits. To become a member, one will undergo two years formation program where one will be guided and directed focusing the interior self that with God's grace and with our Lady's help one may advance and hope to be transformed into the likeness of God. There is our Lady's assurance that she will never stop helping and interceding for each member to obtain God's grace that one will be spiritualized into the likeness of our Lord and Lady.

Community rules will be provided for every professed member as a constant check list to ensure one's life is governed by the holy Presence of the Triune God. Adherence and obedience to the community rules is meritorious and absolutely pleasing to our Lady and to the most Holy Trinity.

Once the member made its profession, he or she in obedience to its superior will do missionary works in accordance to the capability and capacity of the member. Such missionary works includes going into Catholic Churches to enshrine our Lady of Unity if it was not done.

Each professed member will participate in making its home a place to enshrine Our Lady of Unity and to made known to others the existence of her Religious Order and to invite and encourage others to join the Order of our Lady. Interested parties may be invited so they may be introduce to the way of life desired by our Lady and Lord. Professed member should share the book, "Our Lady of Unity" so they will know about the Order. With the copy of "The Last Testament" the professed member should study diligently and share to others for better understanding why we should cultivate and nurture that special relationships with the Triune God. We do commonly heard that a Christian should have a personal relationship with our Lord Jesus Christ but let it be known that God will be honored, exalted and glorified thrice if one have a truly intimate relationship with the Blessed Trinity. Such intimacy with the Triune God made Mary great and blessed that she could never be separated from them. Mary's intimacy with the Holy Trinity compelled her to give God the greatest love a creature could ever give to its Maker. Thus, our Lady was exceedingly exalted way above any creature God made. It is also our Lady's desire that each member will be exalted in accordance to one's love and His will.

It will be the mission of each professed member to make known the greatness of our Lady's intercession to God that it is much wiser and better to have both Jesus and Mary to be on our side since the salvation of our soul is not an easy matter. Yes, our salvation is free but one must know that there are requirements and obligations in fulfilling such free gift contrary to what false teachers preached and taught. It is a fact that billions of souls does not value or in need of our Lady's help and it will be our mission to made known that their chances increases if they seek her help in obtaining that precious grace of salvation. True, Jesus alone is our salvation but let us never forget that He gave us His mother for a reason greater than our own. On the other side of the coin, billions were convinced by our Lady's grand and glorious appearance at Fatima, Portugal where she asked devoted followers and believers to promote in the world devotion to her Immaculate Heart. By doing so, many souls were converted to the true faith and souls were saved from the grasp of hell. This is the power given and entrusted to our Lady so she can minister making her Son's greatest partner in saving souls. And as a professed member of her community, one is responsible in drawing others so that they too can participate with our Lady's mission so the whole world will know her as God's greatest laborer and helper. Imagine that there are still billions of souls who have no clue about our Lady whose greatest desire was to become our mother so she can help us reached our heavenly home. Jesus greatest gift to us was His very Own mother and to reject or ignore her is much like rejecting and ignoring Him. Again, repeating that on the foot of the cross, our Lord gave us not only Himself but also His very Own mother.

"Son behold your mother."

Jesus had to give our Lady for our greatest good knowing how hard and difficult it is to reach our heavenly homeland. He knew that He alone is the Redeemer and Savior of the world but Jesus also knew that her mother will be her greatest helper and partner in completing God's will. We must receive and we should embrace and accept her for she is our greatest inheritance.

And it is for this reason that our Lady of Unity is always calling us to participate in the mission of assisting her in making known of her maternal role and concern for those who have no idea that she too was called just for our sake. She wanted all of us to call on her not because for her own honor and glory but for own honor and glory as adopted children of God.

"Help me help you, this humbly I ask of you."

Our mother's pleading was for you and me. She had all the honors and accolades that will make everyone jealous but she in her perfect humility never seek nor want any part of that for she was full of love for her God and that everything that is not of God was and is rubbish to her. The single reason why she wants us to call on her so she can become a servant to us so in return we too can become a great servant to the Triune God. Thus, her pleading to us was nothing else but to help us get to heaven.

Unfortunately and sadly, there are also millions of Christians who strongly embraced her Son Jesus but critical of His church for its devotion and dedication to the Blessed Virgin Mary and even condemning the true church of idolatry and heresy because of their straightforwardness that only through Jesus Christ alone one will be save. There was and is never any argument about such absolute truth about Jesus but it was the will of God that we do embrace and accept her as our very own mother for Mary was ordained to be our greatest helper and intercessor.

Once again, we are reminded what God showed us at the wedding at Cana.

"They have no more wine."

Notice carefully what Mary said. She did not asked Jesus to provide for the wedding guest but He did as a preview what power Mary had in helping us. It does not need a great theologian to figure how truly powerful is her influenced.

If you have the great Lady in your side she will work hard, she will fight and she will keep pleading for your salvation like a mother hen protecting her brood from the vicious attacks of predators. Having her on your side is the most brilliant lawyer defending your case in judgement day.

Just a final serious thought on our judgement. This revelation is an illustration how God's judgement is so different from ours.

There was a Christian Protestant pastor who labored most of his life preaching and teaching the gospel and he did well on his vocation and all who knew him had no doubt that he was certain for salvation because of his service to our Lord. Once his soul appeared on the judgement throne of Jesus, the divine scale of his justice was tilting towards eternal damnation since the real motive of his ministry was to have a secure and comfortable way of livelihood and his service to God was not truly to glorify Him nor he was truly concern for the salvation of souls. Unfortunately, he had also a hidden life contrary to what he was preaching and teaching. Our Lord Jesus always full of mercy and love was hesitant in sending the pastor to hell knowing that although his motives were impure he still did some good for those who heard his preaching. Our Lord then turn to His mother knowing she would intervene or even give some slight hint for this pastor but our Lady sadly lowered her teary eyes for she want to save him and our Lord understood and knew the pastor never did call on her and there were instances that he did attacked and even condemning the Catholic Church of idolatry and superstition because of the statues of our Lady and saints wrongly and maliciously accused the church as satanic for worshipping idols. Had he receive and honor Mary as his very own mother he would have received that powerful help and Jesus could not refuse.

In a very different scenario, another revelation about a murderer who blamed God for all his miseries and misfortune vowed he would never go to Him. He did not care what God will do to him. Everybody had already condemned this man to hell but his mother was so devoted to our Lady that during her lifetime she never missed praying the Holy Rosary every day and went to daily Mass living in poverty but always putting all her trust and confidence to God despite the bad behaviors of her godless son. When this pious woman died, her murderous wicked godless son suddenly became religious shocking many. He went to regular confession turning a new life in the spirit imitating his mother. He prayed the Holy Rosary daily and also went to daily Mass. After one year of his conversion he became seriously ill and died.

Facing Jesus, our Lord knew this man's salvation was assured because our Lady was standing firmly beside him and without even pleading a word to her Son, Jesus understood right away and welcome this penitent to His kingdom.

Those who are so devoted and dedicated to our Lady can testify how the Blessed Virgin Mary helped them in obtaining their needs. The miracles obtained by our Lady from the Blessed Trinity is an endless list but for the skeptics they still could not or never will accept and embrace her as God's greatest gift to us.

Therefore, if one is truly wise why not have Jesus and Mary on your side. We the community will guarantee that you do not lose a thing but gain everything having both the Son and mother.

REFLECTION

"For as the body is one and hath many members, and all the members of that one body, being many, are one body: so also is Christ". (1Corinthians 12:12).

True and real servants of God is community minded. Before Christ establish His church even though He is God did gathered a community specifically His twelve disciples. There was that saying, no man is an island, and followers of God always formed their own community. The Church was established to gather all God's people into His own community for in numbers is strength and power. The more members in the community the more it benefits for each member has diverse talents and gifts. After Peter's fall denying Jesus, he was steadfast and firm thus became the leader of Christ Church. John the beloved who loved his Master than anything else was able to put into words what is God's love. The rest of the twelve had their own talents and gifts making His community stronger and powerful. Although it was Jesus who was the pillar and the power of the community, its members who were lesser and powerless did contributed something for the greater good of His community. And the church with its billions of members became a powerful spiritual machinery providing members a ministry of healing, preaching, praying, teaching, writing and serving those in need. The Church had many priests, deacons, nuns, consecrated religious, bishops and cardinals working as one powerful voice offering their lives and prayers to God and such community became a power to reckon with and as our Lord had said, no power of hell can prevail against it.

With such strength in numbers the church will continue to stand tall providing the much needed light in our world covered with the darkness of sin.

As our Lord Jesus needed His own community, and as His church needed all its members so does Our Lady of Unity is in great need of her community.

PRAYER

Our Lady Unity, full of grace and mother of the church behold them who knows not Christ the Lord your divine Son and show them that you are also their mother by revealing yourself to them. Our Lady full of love obtain from your Son the graces of their conversion and like you did at Fatima make known to those who does not know you that you are also her mother. Gather and draw them to your maternal care and guide them to the Eternal Word so they will know the way, the truth and the life and lead them to everlasting life prepared by the most Holy Trinity. Remember your devoted community and obtain the graces that they will labor fervently and faithfully in our Lord's vineyard. Amen.

CHAPTER SEVENTEEN

FORMATION PROGRAM

FIRST YEAR:

For the serious soul seeking to grow spiritually and union with the Triune God, the community offers such great opportunity by becoming a professed member of the Order dedicated in giving its life to the One who give us life. Anyone interested to join the Order undergoes a two years formation program introducing oneself to a life greater than itself, making the life of God its own. To lose one's life in order to gain the life of God so we can possess eternal happiness in the new heavens.

"For whosoever will save his life shall lose it: but whosoever will lose his life for my sake, the same shall save it." (Luke 9:24).

Such truth cannot be ignored for the one who lives his own will surely loses the life of God. But blessed are those who forsake its own life for the sake of God's life will surely be save. So clear and concise the message and it is up to us to make the choice.

Again, it is worth repeating this calling so we can truly think and meditate of how can we be truly saved.

"He that findeth his life shall lose it; and he that loseth his life for my sake shall find it." (Matthew 10:39).

The Apostle Matthew repeated the message of Luke that the salvation of our soul is indeed a very serious business not to be taken for granted. Do not be deceived nor be cajoled with those preachers and evangelists that salvation is so easy that all we have to do is to accept Jesus as Lord and Savior and believe in Him and one will be save. There is truth to their message but in reality so very far and remote to the fullness of truth. It takes more than that accepting and believing for the life of God can only be acquired by denying our very own so He can take over transforming oneself into God. Thus, it takes a lifetime of struggles and striving for holiness and perfection and such sublime standard can only be achieve by a lifetime of dedication and devotion to God. To believe and accept our Lord as God and Savior is only the beginning and the ending will be determined by how the will of God was done. Simply said, to believe and accept our Lord only opens the door leading to a gruesome journey. Thus, religious community formed themselves together to inspire and encourage each other to make the journey enjoyable and tolerable.

This is the charism of the Order of Our Lady of Unity.

"TO LIVE THE LIFE OF GOD ENTRUSTED TO US WITH OUR LADY AND OUR LORD AS THE STANDARD ALWAYS DOING GOD'S WILL AND NEVER OUR OWN."

Thus, to those who desires to become a professed member of the Order, the first year formation program are as follows:

FIRST CLASS:

Formation Program is once a month 3 hours or less.
Introduction to Religion:
Why we need religion in our lives. All religions basically is the first step into a relationship with the living God. One will be introduced to the three major religions and the minor ones. One will gain some knowledge although limited but it gives important insight why religion is essential and necessary in our lives. Emphasis on the Jewish religion where the major prophets will be discuss and how it shaped God's greatest work. The Islamic religion will be introduced and its origin. Lastly, the Christian religion defining and detailing why the Catholic Church is the most powerful organized religion. Discussion why this one true church bring salvation to the whole world.

SECOND CLASS:

Dissecting the Catholic Church.
There is no salvation save through the Catholic Church. There is no compromising to this truth. During this class detailed examination of

why the Catholic Church is the one true church that brings salvation to the whole human race.

THIRD CLASS:

The External Life.

Examining our lives in the environment we live in. The risk of losing God and heaven when one's focus is in living solely for worldly pleasure and treasure. How to balance our human and spiritual life while setting our highest goal, to obtain God and heaven. Discussion why we becomes His enemy if we are in love with the world. In this class, instruction how we can use the world as our stepping stone a starting point in reaching our heavenly homeland.

FOURTH CLASS:

The Interior Life.

Our devotion and religiousness is a very good start in cultivating our spiritual life but we should be very careful not to be deceived that our external devotion will save our soul. The example set by the Pharisee should warns us about spiritual pride forgetting that the lowly and the humble pleases God the most. It is not our outward show seen by many but the hidden life that God is most please. In this class, the focus is our immortal soul. The state and condition of our internal life is the most important aspect so it can be properly guided and formed according to God's calling that we too can become holy and perfect.

FIFTH CLASS:

Introducing Our Lady.

Studying the life of our Lady. Before she was born. Her birth. Her labors. Emphasizing the great importance of our Lady's role in our salvation. Billions are missing the great opportunity of our Lady's intercessory power in saving our soul. Lessons from the miracles of her apparition all over the world. Explanation why our Lady is the greatest and the hardest laborer in the Lord's vineyard. Why she is the greatest missionary the greatest preacher and the greatest teacher in how we can conform our will to God's.

SIXTH CLASS:

Introducing The Saints.

They are so relevant in our community's formation for they triumph over their human weaknesses, failures and sinfulness. These saints will be our heroes and inspiration in our own spiritual life. Not only that we should start cultivating spiritual friendship with them for they are most willing to welcome us. As part of the church, they never stop interceding for their brothers and sisters who are still struggling and striving in their journey to their heavenly homeland. Most of us have no clue that the Church Triumphant never stop helping us, the Body of Christ or the Church Militant in our difficult and demanding journey so we can successfully join the Church Triumphant who earned their crown. Such knowledge of the saints will surely inspires us to imitate and follow them so we too will receive the reward promised to those who love Him. It will be highly noted in this session how all of them honored, revered and loved our Lady like their very own mother.

SEVENTH CLASS:

Knowing The Father.

It is of the greatest importance to have the deepest knowledge of the First Persona. Emphasis in reading the entire Old Testament so we will have a better insight and better understanding of God' way. Question and answer why did He created us. Why did He destroyed the old heaven. What is this new heaven promises to us. Knowing the Father definitely increases our love and acquiring intimacy with Him and at the same time we learn something about God's personal relationship with His chosen ones.

EIGHT CLASS:

Knowing The Son, The Second Persona.

The whole world knew and heard His Name but in this class Jesus Life will be examined and deeply explored. Everyone loves our Lord for billions of Christians professed their faith as His followers. But if we dug deeper into His Being one will surely fall deeply and fervently in love with Him. It has become a cliche that God loves us that He sent His only begotten son not to condemn the world but to save it. In this session, we examine our relationship with Christ. Do we really and truly love Him? Critical self assessment of our relationship with Him

NINTH CLASS:

Knowing The Holy Spirit, The Third Persona.

The least honored and revered but the greatest and most important function of God since the Holy Spirit will be the One who finishes and completes the works of the Father and the Son. Without Him, The Son would never have been conceived. It was the Holy Spirit who entered into Jesus along with the power of the most High needed for His mission. And when our Lord ascended to the Father He sent the Holy Spirit as His perfect replacement so His Third Persona will be the One who will enlightened us so we can understand His Words and it was the Holy Spirit who gathered all nation proclaiming the new covenant of perfect love.

TENTH CLASS:

Loving The Father.

Having known the Father in the seventh class, focus is on how we can love Him with all our hearts, mind, body, soul and spirit. We examined the love of Abel, Noah, Abraham, Isaac, Jacob, Moses and others so we can learn the intensity and force of their love. By doing so, we learn something special so we can apply it in our lives.

ELEVENTH CLASS:

Loving The Son.

Having known the Son, focus is on how we can truly and really love Him. Love is most easiest and common word to say but in loving Jesus is the most difficult and the most hardest thing to do. We are easily deceived with our very own opinionated assessment contradicting what is real and truth. We do think that we believe and love Him but sad to say we are so far and remote from the truth and reality. Our love for Jesus is so superficial and to truly love Him takes more than words and actions. In this class, we will be disappointed even discouraged with our failures in giving Jesus all our love. In this session, we will learn how we can truly give our love to Him.

TWELVE CLASS:

Loving The Holy Spirit.

Having known Him as the Finisher of His greatest work and who truly dwells in those deserving we should inflame our hearts to love Him just like our love for the Father and the Son. Deeper study why His gifts is so essential and necessary in our spiritual journey and final formation. In this class, we will learn how we can use His gifts in advancing spiritually. In addition, we will learn how the Third Person of God comes into our soul making it His holy temple. How its indwelling unites us to the Holy Trinity.

REFLECTION

"But now thus saith the Lord that created thee, O Jacob, and he that formed thee, O Israel, Fear not: for I have redeemed thee, I have called thee by thy name; thou art mine."

One will have the greatest opportunity to become a saint if he or she is formed by a religious order whose members were consecrated community to the Triune God with our Lady as its patroness and founder. The formation program educates and guides the soul to seek nothing else but God alone. If one is so attached to the world and other things not of God then the formation of its soul will encounter the greatest difficulties in uniting itself to God. But those who are truly serious and have the greatest desire to become a saint will find its formation a challenging call but will the greatest chance to make it because God will give the grace to those who truly loves Him.

Basically, to become a saint is not a matter that one is chosen by God to become one. In our weaknesses, we made excuses that only those chosen by God can become a saint. Such statement is absolutely wrong. We just love other things more than God for the truth of the matter is that He created each one of us to become like Him. He wants us to be saints. If we made excuses that only those who were chosen then you are denying that God is calling you. When God said, "Fear not; for I have redeemed thee, I have called thee by thy name; thou art mine."

It does not take a smart person to understand that we all are called and chosen. Once we were redeemed with God's Life He encourages and inspire us not to fear in responding to His call because He said we belong to Him. "Thou art mine." To make a silly pathetic excuse that you are not chosen to become a saint is simply a rejection of God's love for you have chosen not love Him back. Thus, you have fulfilled your own self prophesy that you were not chosen. The truth is, you chose not to be chosen.

PRAYER

Beloved Lady of our community, God formed us in our mother's womb and in our lives we inherited that sinful nature making us His enemy. The whole creation rejoiced hearing your fiat knowing that the conqueror of sin and death will come from your blessed womb so He will deliver us from our slavery from sin and death. Beloved mother full of mercy and love, pray for us children of your community that we will always be faithful and true in serving the Holy Trinity through you. Cease not interceding that we who responded your call will obtain that special grace that we be transformed in your likeness so God will be most pleased with us that we may be made worthy to become a saint for His greater honor and glory. Amen.

CHAPTER EIGHTEEN
• •
FORMATION PROGRAM

SECOND YEAR

In phase two of our Lady's formation program as follows:

CLASS THIRTEEN:

Serving God.

Explaining what is the real meaning of serving God and how to give our best in doing it. Discerning one's calling. First and foremost our calling is to accomplish His will in us. Each one of us have different kinds of gift and talents. It is our responsibility to find out what they are and to use it not only for self but for God's greatest glory in serving others. If one is called to the religious life or the secular life, this class will discuss how to maximize its vocation so it can give the greatest glory and honor to the Triune God.

CLASS FOURTEEN:

Serving Neighbor.

Who is then my neighbor? This is the question that every one of us should ponder. In this class the answer will be provided teaching us how we can perfectly fulfill God's second greatest commandment in whatever vocation chosen. Serving our neighbor not only pleases God but also proves our love for Him. Acquiring the knowledge of how we can perfectly love our neighbor will promote spiritual growth advancing it to our ultimate goal.

CLASS FIFTEEN:

Serving Self.

In our spiritual warfare three well known enemies of our salvation are as follows; the world we live in. The devil who never stop hounding and destroying our soul. The flesh which never stop corrupting and ultimately destroying us. A great theologian and saint taught that our greatest enemy is not the world nor the devil but rather us. Our own flesh will never stop fighting our spirit trying to corrupt and kill our soul. He added that once we conquer our own flesh we have also conquered the world and the devil. In this class, we are taught how to conquer self.

CLASS SIXTEEN:

Our Transformation:

In this class, we examine how God transform us into like Him. We trace from the beginning when we were dust. We will know the process of our transforming journey. The beginning of one's life. From our own infancy, to adolescent, adulthood and to old age. An explanation why that no moment in our lives were ever wasted even though we thought they were. Every single moment in our life is a transforming process where we are brought into a defining period or point where the Potter never stop in molding the clay into His desired design. This session reveals that our unpleasant exile is not really bad but in reality is for our greatest good. In our lives we encounter all kinds of agent of our transformation. Each agent is God's gift and grace propelling us to outgrow our humanity fulfilling God's design into the final phase of completing His masterpiece. Detailed examination of the following agents such as our parents, environment, religion, life's experiences and every single happenings. Our world and its mechanism.

CLASS SEVENTEEN:

Recollection Of One's Life.

In order to properly assessed our lives both exterior and interior, this session will assist in evaluating everything in our lives. Great is the need to recollect what was in our past. All of us are sick soul. If we were healthy, our Lord Jesus would have never come to heal us. Everyone of us is a wounded soul and to deny this truth would jeopardize the healing power of God. We have been wounded although our wounds are not the same, nonetheless we are all wounded warriors. Such wounds are never healed specially those deep ones we received in our lifetime for they are imbedded in our soul. Our Lord's mission was to provide healing to those wounds restoring our soul's health. Thus in this session, an in deep examination of self will be the focus of the class. By doing so, we will know better who we are.

CLASS EIGHTEEN:

Period Of Reconciliation.

Solutions are presented as to how we can make that peaceful reconciliation with God. The prodigal son, Mary Magdalene, the good thief, Paul and Peter's reconciling moves will be studied, analyze and discussed as our model on how we can truly be reconciled to God. We cannot deny that we are always in enmity with Him and in this class will be taught how we can truly become friends and not His enemy. Our peaceful reconciliation with Him will be our greatest move so we can start advancing to the next spiritual level.

CLASS NINETEEN:

The Birth Of A New Life.

Once peace with God was made, the Holy Spirit will enter into activity as the enforcer of His graces. The Holy Spirit will give the gifts of wisdom, understanding, knowledge, counsel, piety, fortitude and the fear of the Lord. This gifts will be our tools in discerning what is God's will and what is ours. In this class, discussion about the Holy Spirit active and powerful involvement of the birth of our new life. The birth of Jesus in Mary's womb was made possible by the powerful involvement of the Holy

Spirit and also through Him we receive the newness of life — the life of the Spirit. Thus, the soul is on the way to the new promised land — the new heavens.

CLASS TWENTY:

A Devout Life.

The beginning of this new life creates constant conflict as Scriptures warns us about the war between flesh and spirit. The flesh wants to be catered and to fulfill its unending desires. But the spirit wants the death of the flesh so it will thrive and live to the fullness of its life. In this class, discussion about why the devout life is so demanding and difficult. This is the point where one will be tested and tried revealing one's resolve to live a devout life dedicated solely for God and not self. In the devout life, the soul have no other object but to be near and closer to God as possible in accordance to one's effort and with the help of His grace. This is the determining moment to advance or to withdraw. In this session, will be taught how the Holy Spirit plays the greatest role in giving us fortitude where we never give up in our pursuit of God.

CLASS TWENTY ONE:

A Prayerful Life.

With His gift of fortitude, the Holy Spirit is now operating inspiring the soul to keep on advancing suggesting the soul to pray constantly and unceasingly. A devout life will not be sustained without the power of prayers. It is the essential fuel so one will have the energy and power to thread the narrow path that leads to true life. In this class, will be analyzed why a prayerful life forces God to provide abundant graces to the one who prayed unceasingly. Sacred Scripture revealed how our Lord Jesus prayed unceasingly. And His mother also never stop praying. As member of the Order, we need also to imitate our Lady who prayed unceasingly for us. She is the master of contemplation of the Word of God by keeping it in her heart. Even at the foot of the cross, afflicted with the greatest sorrow and pain, she prayed for the two thieves who were about to die and who are to be judged. By doing so, she succeeded in the conversion of the good thief and for his salvation. A prayerful life is not an option in the community but it is essential and so necessary for the greatest good of our soul and also for the good of the community but most of all we give Him the greatest honor and glory.

CLASS TWENTY TWO:

A Mortified Life.

Having reached this point of our formation, the member will be introduced to a mortified life where the soul is prepared to embrace the life of Christ to perfection. By doing so, and with the help of His grace the soul will be united to the unfathomable and unreachable God. Unlike the building of the tower of Babel where humanity tried their way to reach and see God, we the member should focus on our Lord's teaching that we can never reach and see God with our own efforts. It is the combination of our greatest and sincerest effort and His grace that one can reach that spiritual heights desired by all those saints who made it. But even though we keep failing, the secret of succeeding is to never give up on the resolution to keep climbing the lofty spiritual heights for in doing so, God pleased by our sincere efforts and desire will actively enter with us thus making possible in achieving our goal. Therefore, a mortified life is nothing else but the death of our will and the resurrected life belongs to God. One must lose his life in order to gain His.

CLASS TWENTY THREE:

Labor Of Love.

The Order of our Lady focuses in helping her and her Son in drawing as many soul possible for their conversion and salvation. To labor for love. What our Lord and our Lady loves will also be our passion. They both labored tirelessly and endlessly for the salvation of souls and this will be our work. To labor in our Lord's vineyards in partnership with our Lady to help others in saving their souls. This is what our Lady of Unity's goal and purpose, the salvation of all souls.

CLASS TWENTY FOUR:

Preparation For Profession.

Congratulations. The Lord had chosen you because you chose to respond to His calling by joining and participated in the formation program of the Order of Our Lady of Unity. You chose that His holy will be done to you. Like our Lady's response, "I am the handmaid of the Lord let it be done according to His will."

Schedule for profession and consecration will be celebrated during Holy Mass after certification of the successful candidates. Ring size will be measured in preparation of the solemn ceremony. Books belonging to the Order will be given to the professed member.

REFLECTION

"My little children, of whom I travail in birth again until Christ be formed in you." (Galatians 4:19).

Our Lady whom Christ was formed will be our formation director. No theologians, priests, spiritual masters or gurus can compare with our Lady's direction in how the soul can be perfected into the likeness of her Son. It was our Lady with the fullness of God's graces that she shared God's perfect direction to the God man. Yes, Jesus as God knew the way, the truth and the life and He is our supreme spiritual director but let us not forget the human side of Jesus who is just like us but sin. Despite His sinless nature, our Lady or His mother did her duty perfectly in nurturing, nourishing the humanity of God by feeding Him the Word of God. Although the Word was made flesh and dwelling with us, our Lady as the perfect mother and model of humanity fully feed the human Jesus and when He started His ministry the Word of God became the way of His life showing and teaching His disciples that activating His Words will transform us into God's likeness. Despite the greatest value and importance of God's Word, Jesus showed us the necessity and essentiality of baptism as another important aspect in our salvation. Even John the Baptist was puzzled why Jesus sinless volunteered for baptism and when he saw the Holy Spirit (dove) descended on Him, John understood that as Head of the coming formation of His true Church so must its members will likewise do the same as their Head. An important reminder that after He accomplished His mission and ready to go back to the Father in heaven, He commanded His disciples to baptize everyone by invoking the Triune God's Name.

In our Lady's community, the formation program if one follows it to perfection and with love she promised and guaranteed that in the next life we will have eternal happiness beyond our imagination and expectation.

PRAYER

Holy Mary mother of God who formed the Word into our humanity do obtain for us the grace of fortitude and final perseverance in our desire to be transformed into the likeness of your Son. Remember, Our Lady that we are yours do plead to the most Holy Trinity that He will never permit us to be separated from His Three Persona and from you who formed us into a community devoted and dedicated to the Most High God. As you are perfectly and eternally united with the Blessed Trinity do obtain for us the grace that we members of your community will be united with Him now and forever. Amen.

CHAPTER NINETEEN

THE RULES

The rules of the Order are never to restrict anyone's freedom or to shackle and bind but to give the fullest freedom so the soul will soar to the highest sanctified life. Perfect obedience to the rules is the fastest way to become a saint. Disobedience to the rules not only stunted spiritual growth but will encounter much difficulties in its journey to our heavenly homeland. Therefore, to please the Blessed Trinity, the professed member should at all times vigilant in obeying the Order's rules.

The Rules of the Order as follows:

1. Perfect obedience to the Ten Commandments of God. The professed member should memorized and kept it in the heart.
2. Pray the Holy Rosary daily.
3. Attendance of community meeting every month. Excuse can be made in extremely difficult circumstances.
4. Read and meditate Sacred Scriptures daily spending at least ten minutes.
5. Attendance of Holy Mass on Sundays and holy obligation prescribed by the church. If possible attend daily Mass. Strive to become a daily communicant.
6. After receiving Holy Communion, pray the consecration prayer to the Blessed Trinity.
7. Professed member should go to confession every month or every time a serious sin was committed.

8. Professed member have the option to become a member of SOS Missionaries dedicated in preaching and teaching the Last Testament revealing the works of the Triune God.

9. Professed member should enthrone in their residence portrait of Our Lady of Unity.

10. Member should visit the Blessed Sacrament at least once a week at their most convenient time meditating on our mission. Stay at least fifteen minutes. If possible frequent visits with no time restraint.

11. Member should obey the teachings and precepts of the Catholic Church and of course, obedience to the Pope and the clergy.

12. If possible, volunteer your service to the church when there is a need.

13. A member should strive to live imitating our Lord and our Lady's life by always doing God's will.

14. Member should embrace and practice the virtue of humility for God always resist the proud and exalt the lowly.

15. Member should embrace and practice the virtue of poverty. By doing so, the impurities of our worldly desires will be purified. Resist the temptation and urge to acquire material things that is not truly needed. By acquiring this virtue to perfection the spirit of detachment will make one advance rapidly in its spiritual growth. Highly noted that attachment to material things diminishes one's love for God since our tiny heart will have no more space for the Beloved. Our Lord and Lady lived in simple poverty and even complete detachment from this life and the world.

16. To embrace and practice the virtue of chastity. We all are afflicted with all kinds of impurities in our hearts, minds and soul and member should be very vigilant in guarding what we say, what we do and what we think.

17. To practice and embrace the virtue of meekness preferring patience and fortitude over our selfish emotion. Anger is a very deadly sin but the practice of meekness and patience are the perfect remedy in managing and controlling this deadly sin.

18. To practice and embrace the virtue of generosity exemplified by our Lord and Lady. They were extremely generous in giving themselves completely to God. Helping others specially the truly needy is the standard. Professed member by giving themselves completely to God satisfied this requirement.

19. Never envy anyone. One displeases God when we do for it was ordained that all the gifts, blessings and graces dispensed to others was His will. He made the rich and the poor, the weak and the powerful. He made the beautiful and the less attractive. The good and the bad. To complain that we do not have much and others have more certainly is displeasing to Him. To conquer envy or jealousy, the virtue of brotherly love must constantly be practice to perfection. If someone is a brilliant doctor making so much money and we are struggling to pay our bills give thanks to God that this doctor was blest.

20. Be always active and industrious in everything you do. Wither at work or at home. Do not seek much comfort nor too much leisure and rest. Keep yourself busy working diligently in taking great care of your immortal soul and applying the Order rules in your daily life.

21. Be a servant to all. Serve those who are truly in need specially those who are spiritually bankrupt who had no idea about God and their purpose with their lives. The greatest service we can give to God and neighbor is our service to our brothers and sisters deprived of God's light and grace.

22. Lastly and most importantly member should live a life full of love always for love because only in loving purely and perfectly one will become like God.

23. Finally, be holy and be perfect for this is what God wants us to be by praying unceasingly.

24. May the Most Holy Trinity bless you, keep you, preserve you with His grace through the intercession of Our Lady of Unity, our Foundries.

REFLECTION

"And as many as walk according to this rule, peace be on them, and mercy, and upon the Israel of God." (Galatian 6:16).

St. Teresa of Avila, the famous Carmelite nun and Doctor of the Church emphasized to her community that to become a saint is simply obeying the rules of their community. There is no need to be a great evangelist, preacher, missionary or martyr for the faith to become a saint but by simply obedience to the rules of the Order. By doing so, one obeyed God and His love, peace and mercy will accompany the member in its journey to heaven and God.

Such assurance from this great Carmelite saint should inspire professed member to live its life in perfect obedience to our Lady of Unity's community rules. Each single rules is not a restriction of one's freedom but rather having the greatest freedom from the slavery of sin and to our worldly selfish attachments. St. Therese, the Little Flower also became a great saint and even became a Doctor of the Church doing nothing else inside the enclosed convent as her fellow sister described Therese life. She became a great saint simply because of her love and perfect obedience to the rule of the community. A very simple and easy to do but greatly magnified in God's eyes. On the other hand, disobedience is also magnified. Although she dislike to scrub the floor Therese was always obedient whatever her superior commanded her to do. And all the little small things she did in the convent Therese did it for love. Simply, Therese life in the convent was nothing spectacular or anything great but she became a great Carmelite saint and even became the Patron Saint for Missionaries for her vocation was love.

In closing, we children of Our Lady of Unity should put love above anything else for this is God's holy will.

END